'...sing a song that old was sung...
To glad your ear and please your eyes.
It hath been sung at festivals,
And ember-eves and holy-ales;
And lords and ladies in their lives
Have read it for restoratives.'

William Shakespeare, from Pericles Prince of Tyre

To Cassandra and Edmund

SET THE ECHOES FLYING

Illustrated by Mary Tyler

Published by Fisher Press, Post Office Box 41,
Sevenoaks, Kent TN15 6YN, England

First published in 1997
Compilation copyright © Fisher Press 1997
Illustrations copyright © Mary Tyler 1997

All rights reserved

No part of this publication may be reproduced, stored in a retrieval system, or transmitted, in any form or by any means, electronic, mechanical, photocopying, recording or otherwise, without the prior permission of Fisher Press.

The book is sold subject to the condition that it shall not, by way of trade or otherwise, be lent, re-sold, hired out or otherwise circulated, without the publisher's prior consent in any form of binding or cover other than in which it is published and without a similar condition being imposed on the subsequent purchaser.

British Library Cataloguing in Publication Data
A catalogue record for this book is available from the British Library

ISBN 1 874037 14 0

Printed by Bookcraft (Bath) Ltd., Midsomer Norton
Cover: Sol Communications Ltd., London

CONTENTS

Acknowledgements	vi
Introduction	vii
THE EVER-RUNNING YEAR	1
LITTLE JINGLES, LITTLE CHIMES	23
TO EVERYTHING THERE IS A SEASON	33
A PEACOCK WITH A FIERY TAIL	55
NIGHT AND DAY, BOTH SWEET THINGS	69
UP AND DOWN THE WHOLE CREATION	79
BLOW, BUGLE, BLOW	101
THE HORNS OF ELFLAND FAINTLY BLOWING	125
PUT ON THE WHOLE ARMOUR	145
SHE IS MY COUNTRY STILL	167
OVER THE HILLS AND FAR AWAY	181
I WHISTLE AND I SING	195
BEHOLD, I SHEW YOU A MYSTERY	209
Index of First Lines	238
Index of Authors	245

ACKNOWLEDGEMENTS

We are grateful to Susanna and John, and Joanna and Jamie, who provided the seed corn from which this anthology grew. Without their inspiration it would never have come to fruition. We also wish to thank Ken Richardson, who encouraged us to widen the scope of the book.

Inspiration also came from Coventry Patmore's anthology, *A Child's Garland*, first published in 1861, which was the first of its kind to be based on what children actually liked themselves, rather than what adults thought that they should like.

We also thank Mary and Nick Thompson, founders of The Magnificat Youth Club and Rag Bag Magazine, who have continued to pass on the heritage we celebrate here to young people in Surrey.

INTRODUCTION

This is a collection of poems, songs and hymns which have entertained and inspired those living in England, Ireland, Scotland and Wales during five and a half centuries. Selection has been made from work which has achieved lasting popularity. Over time popularity has a relationship to quality, although not all pieces selected will be equally admired by all at any particular time. We have felt it right to include some work which is not in every respect to our own current taste. Time winnows poems, songs and hymns before they are accepted as classics. While particular pieces go in and out of fashion in the light of contemporary sentiment and interests, the best pieces remain bright in the collective consciousness.

The authors included here are those who lived and died before the early nineteen-twenties. This time scale means that many poets much-loved in our time, such as Kipling, Hardy, Belloc, Chesterton, Eliot, Graves, Houseman and Noyes, are not represented here, nor are more recent poets. Time has not yet winnowed their work. A selection from them is for a later anthology.

Because it is a selection, we could not avoid omitting some favourites. Often this is because the author is better represented by another piece, or because there is a poem by some other author on the same subject which fits the collection better. Wordsworth is well-represented, but his poem on daffodils—currently often voted the most popular poem in the language—is not included. A poem by Robert Herrick on the same subject has been chosen instead.

But the collection is truly comprehensive. It includes much verse treasured by children in every generation; poems which tell a story, amuse, point a moral, stimulate the imagination or reveal a writer's profoundest thoughts. It includes pieces intended to be set to music, as well as some written to be recited or read aloud. We hope this work will encourage a revival of learning by heart. This was common practice, even a few years ago. Imagination, as well as memory skills, will be the poorer if we do not revive that tradition.

The book has been divided into sections. These broadly cover the rhythm of the seasons and their festivals; rhymes which teach, amuse or train the mind; the course of human life, the worlds of the imagination and fantasy; the cycle of day and night; the natural world, the moral struggle, the joys of work, the love of home, and of travel and pilgrimage. It concludes with a section on the mystery of existence, with special emphasis on the orthodox Christian tradition, which has been the major formation and inspiration for writers throughout the period. Those who seek out poems and songs which emphasise the hopelessness and futility of life, are likely to find this anthology depressingly cheerful and upbeat: although it does not shy away from death, in the main it celebrates the joys of life.

We have not included translations from other languages, except in the case of the Bible, and of some pieces, originally in Welsh, which have established themselves in English in their own right. The Bible text used is the King James' version. This was not traditionally used by Catholics, and, in recent years, it has been partially superseded by other versions, even among Anglicans. Yet it is the one which has been most influential in the English language literary tradition. Most work is by authors from the British Isles. But a few North American poets have slipped in whose pieces have been 'naturalised' in these islands. Spelling and vocabulary have not been modernised in Chaucer, nor in the mediæval poems, songs and hymns: the sense is usually clear from the context. But the spelling of Shakespeare's verse, and that of the 15th, 16th, 17th and 18th century pieces has been standardised. The accepted spelling of Scottish English has been used. There are notes only where allusions demand particular explanation. There is a general assumption that readers are resourceful!

The book is for all ages: boys and girls, women and men. The joy which the editors have had in compiling it is enhanced by the conviction that it will also bring joy to others who have, or will acquire, a love of this great inheritance.

THE EVER-RUNNING YEAR

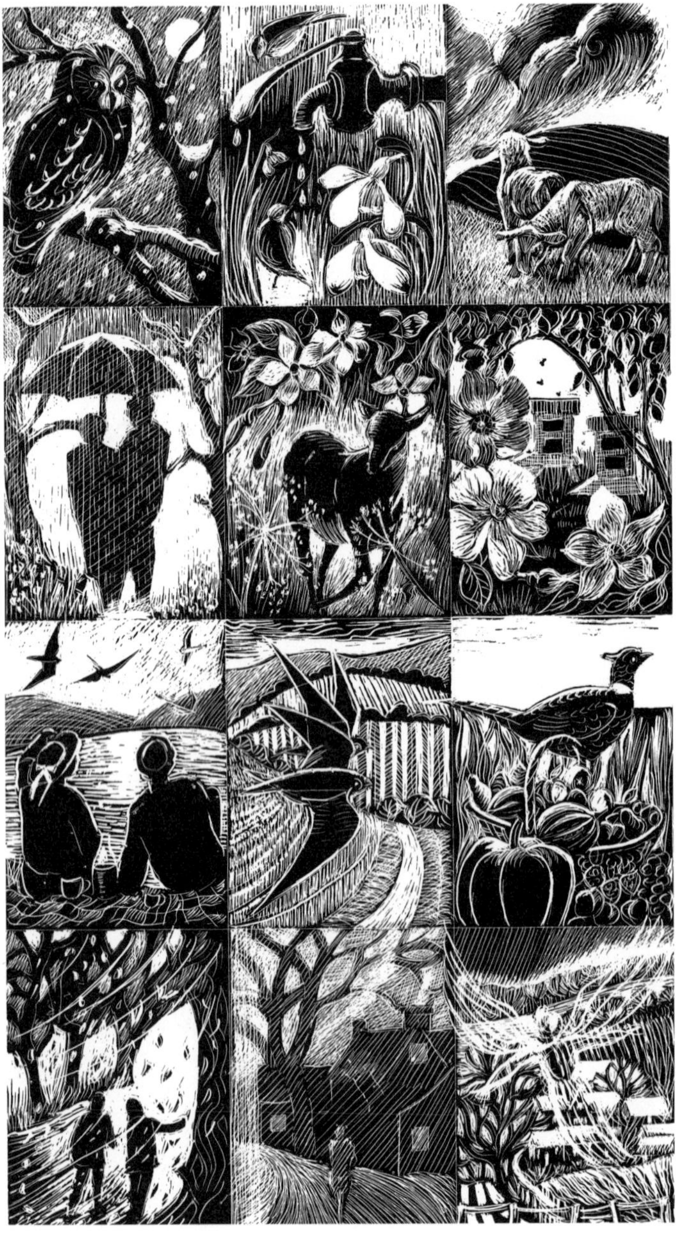

COLD WEATHER

FIRST it rained, and then it snew,
Then it friz, and then it thew,
   And then it friz again.

Traditional

WINTER

WHEN icicles hang by the wall,
   And Dick the shepherd blows his nail,
And Tom bears logs into the hall,
And milk comes frozen home in pail,
When blood is nipp'd, and ways be foul,
Then nightly sings the staring owl:
'Tu-who!
Tu-whit, Tu-who!'—A merry note,
While greasy Joan doth keel the pot.

When all aloud the wind doth blow,
And coughing drowns the parson's saw,
And birds sit brooding in the snow,
And Marian's nose looks red and raw,
When roasted crabs hiss in the bowl,
Then nightly sings the staring owl:
'Tu-who!
Tu-whit, Tu-who!'—A merry note,
While greasy Joan doth keel the pot.

William Shakespeare, from Love's Labour's Lost

CHRISTMAS IS COMING

CHRISTMAS is coming, the geese are getting fat,
Please put a penny in an old man's hat.
If you haven't got a penny, a ha'penny will do,
If you haven't got a ha'penny, God bless you!

Traditional

A CHRISTMAS CAROL

IN the bleak mid-winter
  Frosty wind made moan,
Earth stood hard as iron,
  Water like a stone;
Snow had fallen, snow on snow,
  Snow on snow,
In the bleak mid-winter
    Long ago.

Our God, Heaven cannot hold Him
  Nor earth sustain;
Heaven and earth shall flee away
  When He comes to reign:
In the bleak mid-winter
  A stable-place sufficed
The Lord God Almighty
    Jesus Christ.

Enough for Him, whom cherubim
  Worship night and day,
A breastful of milk
  And a mangerful of hay;
Enough for Him, whom angels
  Fall down before,
The ox and ass and camel
    Which adore.

Angels and archangels
  May have gathered there,
Cherubim and seraphim
  Thronged the air;
But only His mother
  In her maiden bliss
Worshipped the Beloved
    With a kiss.

What can I give Him,
  Poor as I am?
If I were a shepherd
  I would bring lamb,
If I were a Wise Man

I would do my part,—
Yet what I can I give Him,
 Give my heart.

Christina Rosetti

I SING OF A MAIDEN

I SING of a maiden
 That is makeless;
King of all kings
 To her son she ches.

He came all so still
 Where His mother was,
As dew in April
 That falleth on the grass. *(chorus)*

He came all so still
 To His mother's bower,
As dew in April
 That falleth on the flower. *(chorus)*

He came all so still
 Where His mother lay,
As dew in April
 That falleth on the spray. *(chorus)*

Mother and maiden
 Was never none but she;
Well may such a lady
 Goddes mother be. *(chorus)*

15th century carol

LULLAY, MY LIKING

I SAW a fair maiden
 Sitten and sing:
She lullèd a little child,
 A sweetè lording.

 Lullay my liking, my dear son, my sweeting;
 Lullay my dear heart, mine own dear darling!

That eternal lord is He
    That made allè thing;
Of allè lordès He is Lord,
    Of allè kingès King: *(chorus)*

There was mickle melody
    At that childès birth:
Although they were in heaven's bliss
    They madè mickle mirth: *(chorus)*

Angels bright they sang that night
    And saiden to that child:
'Blessed be Thou, and so be she
    That is both meek and mild': *(chorus)*

Pray we now to that child,
    And to His mother dear,
Grant them all His blessing
    That now maken cheer: *(chorus)*

15th century carol

A HYMN OF THE NATIVITY

VERSES SUNG BY THE SHEPHERDS

WELCOME, all wonders in one sight!
    Eternity shut in a span!
Summer in Winter! Day in Night!
    Heaven in earth, and God in man!
Great little One! whose all-embracing birth
Lifts Earth to Heaven, stoops Heaven to Earth!

Welcome, tho' not to gold nor silk,
    To more than Caesar's birthright is;
Two sister seas of virgin milk,
    With many a rarely-temper'd kiss,
That breathes at once both maid and mother,
Warms in the one, cools in the other.

She sings Thy tears asleep, and dips
    Her kisses in Thy weeping eye;
She spreads the red leaves of Thy lips,
    That in their buds yet blushing lie.

She 'gainst those mother-diamonds tries
The points of her young eagle's eyes.

Welcome—tho' not to those gay flies,
   Gilded i' th' beams of earthly kings;
Slippery souls in smiling eyes—
   But to poor shepherds, homespun things;
Whose wealth's their flocks, whose wit, to be
Well-read in their simplicity.

Yet, when young April's husband show'rs
   Shall bless the fruitful Maia's bed,
We'll bring the first born of her flowers,
   To kiss Thy feet, and crown Thy head.
To thee, dread Lamb! whose love must keep
The shepherds, more than they their sheep.

To Thee, meek Majesty, soft King
   Of simple graces and sweet loves:
Each of us his lamb will bring,
   Each his pair of silver doves:
Till burnt at last in fire of Thy fair eyes,
Ourselves become our own best sacrifice.

Richard Crashaw

THE HOLLY AND THE IVY

THE holly and the ivy,
   When they are both full grown,
Of all the trees that are in the wood,
   The holly bears the crown.

   O the rising of the sun,
      And the running of the deer,
   The playing of the merry organ,
      Sweet singing in the choir.

The holly bears a blossom,
   As white as the lily flower;
And Mary bore sweet Jesus Christ,
   To be our sweet Saviour. *(chorus)*

The holly bears a berry,
   As red as any blood;
And Mary bore sweet Jesus Christ
   To do poor sinners good. *(chorus)*

The holly bears a prickle,
   As sharp as any thorn;
And Mary bore sweet Jesus Christ
   On Christmas Day in the morn. *(chorus)*

The holly bears a bark,
   As bitter as any gall;
And Mary bore sweet Jesus Christ,
   For to redeem us all. *(chorus)*

Traditional Carol

SEE AMID THE WINTER'S SNOW

SEE amid the winter's snow,
Born for us on earth below,
See the tender Lamb appears,
Promised from eternal years!

> *Hail, thou ever-blessèd morn!*
> *Hail Redemption's happy dawn!*
> *Sing through all Jerusalem,*
> *Christ is born in Bethlehem.*

Lo, within a manger lies
He, Who built the starry skies:
He, Who throned in height sublime
Sits amid the Cherubim: *(chorus)*

Say, ye holy Shepherds, say,
What your joyful news today;
Wherefore have you left your sheep
On the lonely mountain steep? *(chorus)*

'As we watched at dead of night,
Lo, we saw a wondrous light;
Angels singing, "Peace on earth,"
Told us of the Saviour's birth.' *(chorus)*

Teach, O teach us, holy Child,
By Thy face so meek and mild,
Teach us to resemble Thee,
In Thy sweet humility! *(chorus)*

Virgin mother, Mary blest,
By the joys that fill thy breast,
Pray for us that we may prove
Worthy of the Saviour's love. *(chorus)*

Edward Caswall

WASSAIL SONG

HERE we come a-wassailing
Among the leaves so green,
Here we come a-wandering,
    So fair to be seen.

Love and joy come to you,
And to you your wassail too,
And God bless you, and send you
A Happy New Year.

We are not daily beggars
    That beg from door to door,
But we are neighbours' children
    Whom you have seen before. *(chorus)*

God bless the master of this house,
    Likewise the mistress too;
And all the little children
    That round the table go; *(chorus)*

And all your kin and kinsfolk,
    That dwell both far and near;
We wish you a Merry Christmas,
    And a Happy New Year. *(chorus)*

Traditional Carol

THE TWELVE DAYS OF CHRISTMAS[1]

ON the first day of Christmas my true love sent to me
A partridge in a pear tree.

On the second day of Christmas my true love sent to me
Two turtle doves, and a partridge in a pear tree.

On the third day of Christmas my true love sent to me
Three French hens, two turtle doves, etc.

On the fourth day of Christmas my true love sent to me:
Four calling birds, three French hens, etc.

On the fifth day of Christmas my true love sent to me:
Five golden rings, four calling birds, etc.

On the sixth day of Christmas my true love sent to me:
Six geese a-laying, five golden rings, etc.

On the seventh day of Christmas, my true love sent to me:
Seven swans a-swimming, six geese a-laying, etc.

On the eighth day of Christmas my true love sent to me:
Eight maids a-milking, seven swans a-swimming, etc.

On the ninth day of Christmas my true love sent to me
Nine ladies dancing, eight maids a-milking, etc.

On the tenth day of Christmas my true love sent to me:
Ten lords a-leaping, nine ladies dancing, etc.

On the eleventh day of Christmas my true love sent to me:
Eleven pipers piping, ten lords a-leaping, etc.

On the twelfth day of Christmas my true love sent to me:
Twelve drummers drumming, eleven pipers piping, etc.

Traditional Carol

---

1. It has become clear that this English Christmas carol was originally used as a means of instructing children and adults in the basic truths of the Catholic Faith during the time when the teaching and practice of the Old Religion were proscribed in Britain (between 1558 and the years leading up to Catholic Emancipation in 1829). The strange gifts of the 'true love'—God— were: the partridge, Jesus Christ, (the bird feigns injury to decoy predators from its nest); the two turtle doves: the Old and New Testaments; the three French hens: Faith, Hope and Charity; the four calling birds: the four Gospels; the five golden rings: the first five books of the Old Testament, which tell of Man's fall from grace; the six geese a-laying: the six days of creation; the seven swans a-swimming: the seven gifts of the Holy Spirit; the eight maids a-milking: the eight Beatitudes; the nine ladies dancing: the nine fruits of the Holy Spirit; the ten lords a-leaping: the Ten Commndments; the eleven pipers piping: the eleven faithful disciples; the twelve drummers drumming: the twelve points of belief in the Apostle's Creed.

CHRISTMAS AT SEA

THE sheets were frozen hard, and they cut the naked hand;
The decks were like a slide, where a seaman scarce could stand;
The wind was nor'wester, blowing squally off the sea;
And cliffs and spouting breakers were the only things a-lee.

They heard the surf a-roaring, before the break of day;
But 'twas only with the peep of light we saw how ill we lay.
We tumbled every hand on deck instanter, with a shout,
And we gave her the maintops'l, and stood by to go about.

All day we tacked and tacked between the South Head and the North;
All day we hauled the frozen sheets, and got no further forth;
All day as cold as charity, in bitter pain and dread,
For very life and nature we tacked from head to head.

We gave the South a wider birth, for there the tide-race roared;
But every tack we made we brought the North Head close aboard;
So's we saw the cliffs and houses, and the breakers running high,
And the coastguard in his garden, with his glass against his eye.

The frost was on the village roofs as white as ocean foam;
The good red fires were burning bright in every 'longshore home;
The windows sparkled clear, and chimneys volleyed out;
And I vow we sniffed the victuals as the vessel went about.

The bells upon the church were rung with mighty jovial cheer,
For it's just that I should tell you how (of all the days in the year)
This day of our adversity was blessèd Christmas morn,
And the house above the coastguard's was the house where I was born.

O well I saw the pleasant room, the pleasant faces there,
My mother's silver spectacles, my father's silver hair;
And well I saw the firelight, like a flight of homely elves,
Go dancing round the china-plates that stand upon the shelves.

And well I know the talk they had, the talk that was of me,
Of the shadow on the household and the son that went to sea;
And O the wicked fool I seemed, in every kind of way,
To be here and hauling frozen ropes on blessèd Christmas Day.

They lit the high sea-light, and the dark began to fall.
'All hands to loose topgallant sails,' I heard the captain call,

'By the Lord, she'll never stand it,' our first mate, Jackson, cried.
…'It's the one way or the other, Mr Jackson,' he replied.

She staggered to her bearings, but the sails were new and good.
And the ship smelt up to windward just as though she understood.
As the winter's day was ending, in the entry of the night,
We cleared the weary headland, and passed below the light.

And they heaved a mighty breath, every soul on board but me,
As they saw her nose again pointing handsome out to sea;
But all that I could think of, in the darkness and the cold,
Was just that I was leaving home and my folks were growing old.

Robert Louis Stevenson

NEW YEAR

RING out, wild bells, to the wild sky,
  The flying cloud, the frosty light:
   The year is dying in the night;
Ring out, wild bells, and let him die.

Ring out the old, ring in the new,
  Ring, happy bells, across the snow:
   The year is going, let him go;
Ring out the false, ring in the true.

Ring out the grief that saps the mind,
  For those that here we see no more;
   Ring out the feud of rich and poor,
Ring in redress to all mankind.

Ring out a slowly dying cause,
  And ancient forms of party strife;
   Ring in the nobler modes of life,
With sweeter manners, purer laws.

Ring out the want, the care, the sin,
  The faithless coldness of the times;
   Ring out, ring out my mournful rhymes,
But ring the fuller minstrel in.

Ring out false pride in place and blood,
  The civic slander and the spite;

Ring in the love of truth and right,
Ring in the common love of good.

Ring out old shapes of foul disease;
   Ring out the narrowing lust of gold;
   Ring out the thousand wars of old,
Ring in the thousand years of peace.

Ring in the valiant man and free,
   The larger heart, the kindlier hand;
   Ring out the darkness of the land,
Ring in the Christ that is to be.

Alfred, Lord Tennyson, from In Memoriam

EPIPHANY

O WORSHIP the Lord in the beauty of holiness!
Bow down before Him, His glory proclaim;
With gold of obedience, and incense of lowliness,
   Kneel and adore him, the Lord is His name!

Low at His feet lay thy burden of carefulness,
   High on His heart He will bear it for thee,
Comfort thy sorrows, and answer thy prayerfulness,
   Guiding thy steps as may best for thee be.

Fear not to enter His courts in the slenderness
   Of the poor wealth thou would'st reckon as thine:
Truth in its beauty, and love in its tenderness,
   These are the offerings to lay on His shrine.

These, though we bring them in trembling and fearfulness,
   He will accept for the name that is dear;
Mornings of joy give for evenings of tearfulness,
   Trust for our trembling and hope for our fear.

John Samuel Bewley Monsell

CANDLEMAS DAY: 2ND FEBRUARY

IF Candelmas be fair and bright,
Winter'll have another flight.
But if Candlemas Day be clouds and rain,
Winter is gone and will not come again.   *Traditional*

LENT

Forty days and forty nights
   Thou was fasting in the wild;
Forty days and forty nights
   Tempted, and yet undefiled:

Sunbeams scorching all the day;
   Chilly dew-drops nightly shed;
Prowling beasts about the way;
   Stones Thy pillow, earth Thy bed.

Shall not we thy watchings share,
   And from earthly joys abstain,
Fasting with unceasing prayer,
   Glad with Thee to suffer pain?

And if Satan, vexing sore,
   Flesh or spirit should assail,
Thou his vanquisher before,
   Grant we may not faint nor fail.

So shall we have peace divine;
   Holier gladness ours shall be;
Round us too shall Angels shine,
   Such as ministered to Thee.

Keep, O keep us, Saviour dear,
   Ever constant by Thy side;
That with Thee we may appear
   At the eternal Eastertide.

George Hunt Smyttan

EASTER

I got me flowers to straw Thy way,
   I got me boughs off many a tree;
But Thou wast up by break of day,
   And brought'st Thy sweets along with Thee.

Yet though my flowers be lost, they say
   A heart can never come too late;
Teach it to sing Thy praise this day,
   And then this day my life shall date.

George Herbert

DESCRIPTION OF SPRING

Wherein each thing renews, save only the Lover

THE soote season, that bud and bloom forth brings,
   With green hath clad the hill and eke the vale.
The nightingale with feathers new she sings;
   The turtle to her make hath told her tale.
Summer is come, for every spray now springs:
The hart hath hung his old head on the pale;
The buck in brake his winter coat he flings;
The fishes fleet with new repairèd scale;
The adder all her slough away she slings;
The swift swallow pursueth the flies smale;
The busy bee her honey now she mings;
Winter is worn that was the flowers' bale.
And thus I see among these pleasant things
Each care decays, and yet my sorrow springs.

Henry Howard, Earl of Surrey

SONG

UNDER the greenwood tree
   Who loves to lie with me,
And turn his merry note
Unto the sweet bird's throat,
Come hither, come hither, come hither.
Here shall he see
No enemy
But winter and rough weather.

William Shakespeare, from As You Like It

SPRING

NOTHING is so beautiful as spring—
   When weeds, in wheels, shoot long and lovely and lush;
     Thrush's eggs look little low heavens, and thrush
Through the echoing timber does so rinse and wring
The ear, it strikes like lightnings to hear him sing;
     The glassy peartree leaves and blooms, they brush
     The descending blue; that blue is all in a rush
With richness; the racing lambs too have fair their fling.

What is all this juice and all this joy?
   A strain of the earth's sweet being in the beginning
In Eden garden.—Have, get, before it cloy,
   Before it cloud, Christ, lord, and sour with sinning,
Innocent mind and Mayday in girl and boy,
   Most, O maid's child, thy choice and worthy the winning.

Gerard Manley Hopkins

SONG

A SUNNY shaft did I behold,
   From sky to earth it slanted:
And poised therein a bird so bold—
   Sweet bird, thou wert enchanted!

He sank, he rose, he twinkled, he trolled
   Within that shaft of sunny mist;
His eyes of fire, his beak of gold,
   All else of amethyst!

And thus he sang: 'Adieu! adieu!
Love's dreams prove seldom true.
The blossoms, they make no delay:
The sparkling dew-drops will not stay.
   Sweet month of May,
     We must away;
    Far, far, away!
      Today! today!'

Samuel Taylor Coleridge

SUMMER

SO, some tempestuous morn in early June,
   When the year's primal burst of bloom is o'er,
     Before the roses and the longest day—
   When garden-walks, and all the grassy floor,
     With blossoms red and white of fallen May
      And chestnut-flowers are strewn—
   So have I heard the cuckoo's parting cry,
     From the wet field, through the vext garden-trees,
     Come with the volleying rain and tossing breeze:
The bloom is gone, and with the bloom go I!

Too quick despairer, wherefore wilt thou go?
   Soon will the high Midsummer pomps come on,
      Soon will the musk carnations break and swell,
Soon shall we have gold-dusted snapdragon,
   Sweet-William with his homely cottage-smell,
      And stocks in fragrant blow;
Roses that down the alleys shine afar,
   And open, jasmine-muffled lattices,
   And groups under the dreaming garden-trees,
And the full moon, and the white evening star.

Matthew Arnold, from Thyrsis

ST SWITHIN'S DAY: 15TH OF JULY

ST Swithin's Day, if thou dost rain,
For forty days it will remain;
St Swithin's day, if thou be fair,
For forty days 'twill rain na mair.

Traditional

CUCKOO

CUCKOO, Cuckoo,
What do you do?
   'In April
I open my bill;
   In May
I sing night and day;
   In June
I change my tune;
   In July
Away I fly;
   In August
Away I must.'

Traditional

THE KITTEN AND FALLING LEAVES

SEE the Kitten on the wall,
Sporting with the leaves that fall,
Withered leaves—one—two—and three—
From the lofty elder-tree!
Through the calm and frosty air
Of this morning bright and fair,
Eddying round and round they sink
Softly, slowly: one might think,
From the motions that are made,
Every little leaf conveyed
Sylph or Faery hither tending,—
To this lower world descending,
Each invisible and mute,
In his wavering parachute.
—But the Kitten, how she starts,
Crouches, stretches, paws and darts!
First at one, and then its fellow,
Just as light and just as yellow;
There are many now—now one—
Now they stop and there are none:
What intenseness of desire
In her upward eye of fire!
With a tiger-leap half way
Now she meets the coming prey,
Lets it go as fast, and then
Has it in her power again:
Now she works with three or four,
Like an Indian conjuror;
Quick as he in feats of art,
Far beyond in joy of heart.
Were the antics played in the eye
Of a thousand standers-by,
Clapping hands with shouts and stare,
What would little Tabby care
For the plaudits of the crowd?
Over happy to be proud,
Over wealthy in the treasure
Of her own exceeding pleasure!…

William Wordsworth—an extract

SONNET SEVENTY-THREE

THAT time of year thou mayst in me behold
When yellow leaves, or none, or few, do hang
Upon those boughs which shake against the cold,
Bare ruin'd choirs where late the sweet birds sang.
In me thou seest the twilight of such day
As after sunset fadeth in the west,
Which by and by black night doth take away,
Death's second self, that seals up all in rest.
In me thou seest the glowing of such fire
That on the ashes of his youth doth lie,
As the death-bed whereon it must expire,
Consum'd with that which it was nourish'd by.
   This thou perceiv'st which makes thy love more strong,
   To love that well which thou must leave ere long.

William Shakespeare

TO AUTUMN

SEASON of mists and mellow fruitfulness;
Close bosom-friend of the maturing sun;
Conspiring with him how to load and bless
   With fruit the vines that round the thatch-eaves run;
To bend with apples the moss'd cottage-trees,
   And fill all fruit with ripeness to the core;
     To swell the gourd, and plump the hazel shells
   With a sweet kernel; to set budding more,
And still more, later flowers for the bees,
Until they think warm days will never cease,
     For Summer has o'er-brimmed their clammy cells.

Who hath not seen thee oft amid thy store?
   Sometimes whoever seeks abroad may find
Thee sitting careless on a granary floor,
   Thy hair soft-lifted by the winnowing wind;
Or on a half-reap'd furrow sound asleep,
   Drows'd with the fume of poppies, while thy hook
     Spares the next swath and all its twinèd flowers:
And sometimes like a gleaner thou dost keep
   Steady thy laden head across a brook;

Or by a cyder-press, with patient look,
　　Thou watchest the last oozings hours by hours.

Where are the songs of Spring? Ay, where are they?
　　Think not of them, thou has thy music too,—
While barrèd clouds bloom the soft-dying day,
　　And touch the stubble-plains with rosy hue;
Then in a wailful choir the small gnats mourn
　　Among the river sallows, borne aloft
　　　　Or sinking as the light wind lives or dies;
And full-grown lambs loud bleat from hilly bourn;
　　Hedge-crickets sing; and now with treble soft
　　The red-breast whistles from a garden croft;
　　　　And gathering swallows twitter in the skies.

John Keats

ODE TO THE WEST WIND

O WILD West Wind , thou breath of Autumn's being,
Thou, from whose unseen presence the leaves dead
Are driven, like ghosts from an enchanter fleeing,

Yellow, and black, and pale, and hectic red,
Pestilence-sticken multitudes: O thou,
Who chariotest to their dark wintry bed

The wingèd seeds, where they lie cold and low,
Each like a corpse within its grave, until
Thine azure sister of the Spring shall blow

Her clarion o'er the dreaming earth, and fill
(Driving sweet buds like flocks to feed in air)
With living hues and odours plain and hill:

Wild Spirit, which art moving everywhere;
Destroyer and preserver; hear, oh, hear!

Thou on whose stream, mid the steep sky's commotion,
Loose clouds like earth's decaying leaves are shed,
Shook from the tangled boughs of Heaven and Ocean,

Angels of rain and lightning: there are spread
On the blue surface of thine aëry surge,
Like the bright hair uplifted from the head

THE EVER-RUNNING YEAR

Of some fierce Maenad, even from the dim verge
Of the horizon to the zenith's height,
The locks of the approaching storm. Thou dirge

Of the dying year, to which this closing night
Will be the dome of a vast sepulchre,
Vaulted with all thy congregated might

Of vapours, from whose solid atmosphere
Black rain, and fire, and hail will burst: oh hear!...

Make me thy lyre, even as the forest is:
What if my leaves are falling like its own!
The tumult of thy mighty harmonies

Will take from both a deep, autumnal tone,
Sweet though in sadness. Be thou, Spirit fierce,
My spirit! Be thou me, impetuous one!

Drive my dead thoughts over the universe
Like withered leaves to quicken a new birth!
And by incantation of this verse,

Scatter, as from an unextinguished hearth
Ashes and sparks, my words among mankind!
Be through my lips to unawakened earth

The trumpet of a prophesy! O, Wind,
If Winter comes, can Spring be far behind?

Percy Bysshe Shelley, part of the Ode

THE TWELVE MONTHS

Snowy, Flowy, Blowy,
   Showery, Flowery, Bowery,
Hoppy, Croppy, Droppy,
   Breezy, Sneezy, Freezy.

George Ellis

LITTLE JINGLES, LITTLE CHIMES

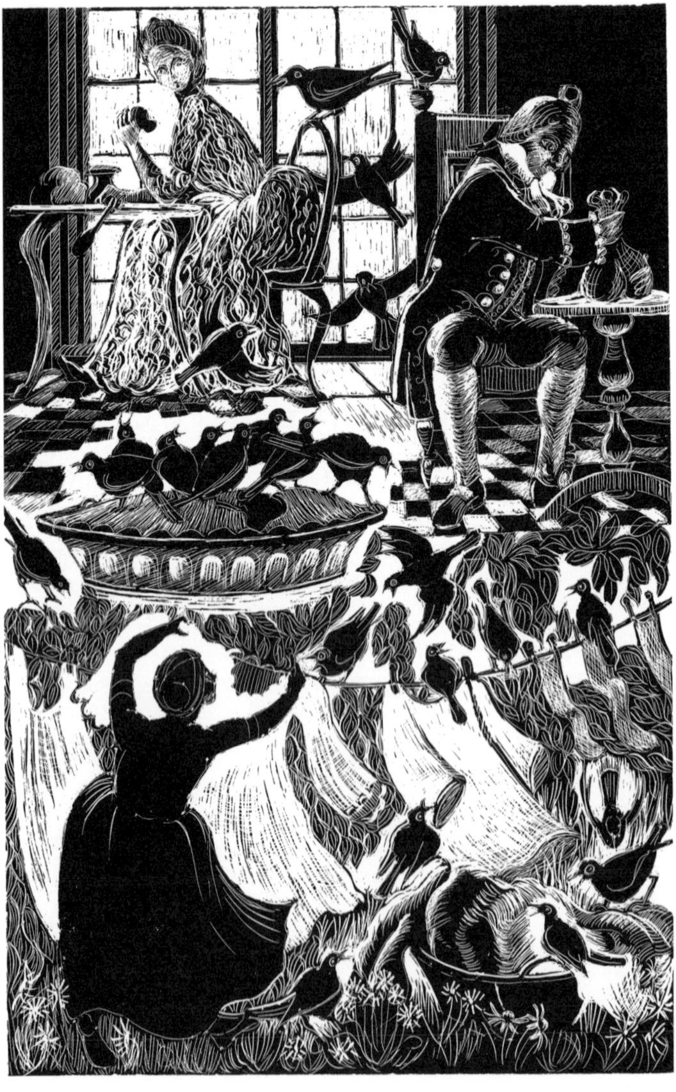

SING A SONG OF SIXPENCE

SING a song of sixpence,
A pocket full of rye,
Four-and-twenty blackbirds
　　Baked in a pie;
When the pie was opened
　　The birds began to sing;
Wasn't that a dainty dish
　　To set before a king?

The king was in his counting-house,
　　Counting out his money,
The queen was in the parlour,
　　Eating bread and honey;
The maid was in the garden,
　　Hanging out the clothes,
Down flew a blackbird
　　And pecked off her nose.

Traditional

YIN TWA THREE

YIN, twa, three;
　Me mither catched a flea.
We roastit it,
And toastit it,
And had it til oor tea!

Scottish traditional

PETALS

ONE I love, two I love,
　Three I love, I say;
Four I love with all my heart,
Five I cast away;
Six he loves,
Seven she loves,
Eight they love together;
Nine he comes, ten he tarries,
Eleven he woos, and twelve he marries.

Traditional

APPLE-PIE

A was an Apple-pie:
  B bit it,
  C cut it,
  D dealt it,
  E eat it,
  F fought for it,
  G got it,
  H had it,
  J joined it,
  K kept it,
  L longed for it,
  M mourned for it,
  N nodded it,
  O opened it,
  P peeped into it,
  Q quartered it,
  R ran for it,
  S stole it,
  T took it,
  V viewed it,
  W wanted it,
  X, Y ,& Z, and all wished for a piece in hand.

Traditional

DON'T CARE

DON'T-CARE—he didn't care;
    Don't-Care was wild.
Don't-Care stole plum and pear
    Like any beggar's child

Don't-Care was made to care,
    Don't-Care was hung;
Don't Care was put in the pot
    And boiled till he was done.

Traditional

RUNAWAY DAUGHTER

ROSY apple, lemon or pear,
Bunch of roses she shall wear;
Gold and silver by her side,
I know who shall be the bride.
Take her by the lily-white hand,
Lead her to the altar;
Give her kisses one, two, three,
Mother's runaway daughter.

Anon

CHERRY STONES

TINKER, tailor,
Soldier, sailor,
Rich man, poor man,
Beggar man,
Thief.

Silk,
Satin,
Calico,
Rags.

House,
Castle
Pigstye,
Barn.

Coach
Carriage
Wheelbarrow
Car.

Traditional

PETER PIPER

PETER PIPER picked a peck of pickled pepper;
A peck of pickled pepper Peter Piper picked;
If Peter Piper picked a peck of pickled pepper,
Where's the peck of pickled pepper Peter Piper picked?

Traditional

WHAT A PICKLE I'M IN

O DEAR me, what a pickle I'm in!
I've lost my pocket handkerchief, and found a double chin;
O dear me! trouble's never done,
I've dropped all my h's and I can't find one.

Anon

BLUE BELLS, COCKLE SHELLS

BLUE bells, cockle shells,
Eeevy, ivy, OVER!
My mother said that I never should
Play with the gypsies in the wood.
If I did then she would say,
'You naughty girl to disobey.'

Traditional

THOMAS A TITTIMUS

THOMAS A TITTIMUS took two T's
To tie them up to two tall trees:
How many T's in that?

Anon

THE MODERN HIAWATHA

WHEN he killed the Mudjokivis,
Of the skin he made him mittens,
Made them with the fur side inside,
Made them with the skin side outside,
He, to get the warm side inside,
Put the inside skin side outside;
He to get the cold side outside,
Put the warm side fur side inside.
That's why he put the fur side inside,
Why he put the skin side outside,
Why he turned them inside outside.

Anon

SHEEP COUNTING

YAN, tan tethera, methera,
Pimp, hata, slata, lowra, dowra, dick.

Otherum, tetherum, cockerum, citherum,
Shitherum, shatherum, viner, wagger, den.

Traditional

MATHS

MULTIPLICATION is vexation,
Division is as bad;
The Rule of Three doth puzzle me
And practice drives me mad!

Anon

MOTOR BUS

WHAT is this that roareth thus?
Can it be a *Motor Bus?*
Yes, the smell and hideous hum
Indicat Motorem Bum!
Implet in the Corn and High
Terror me Motoris Bi:
Bo Motori clamitabo
Ne Motore caedar a Bo—
Dative be or Ablative
So thou only let us live:
Whither shall thy victims flee?
Spare us, spare us, *Motor Be!*
Thus I sang; and still and still anigh
Came in *hordes Motores Bi,*
Et complebat omne forum
Copia Motorum Borum.
How shall wretches live like us
Cincti Bis Motoribus?
Domine, defende nos
Contra hos Motores Bos!

Alfred Dennis Godley

BEES

A SWARM of bees in May is worth a load of hay;
A swarm of bees in June is worth a silver spoon;
A swarm of bees in July is not worth a fly.

Traditional

THE WEATHER

RED sky at night,
Shepherd's delight;
Red sky in the morning,
Shepherd's warning.

Traditional

TREES

IF the oak is out before the ash,
Then you'll only get a splash.
But if the ash beats the oak,
Then you can expect a soak.

Traditional

DAYS IN THE MONTH

THIRTY days hath September,
April, June, and November;
All the rest have thirty-one,
Excepting February alone,
Which has but twenty-eight days clear,
And twenty-nine at each leap year.

Traditional

JUNE WEDDINGS

Same old slippers,
　　Same old rice,
Same old glimpse of
　　Paradise.

William Lampton

THE BELLS OF LONDON

GAY go up and gay go down,
To ring the bells of London town.
Half-pence and farthings,
Say the bells of St Martin's.
   Oranges and lemons,
   Say the bells of St Clement's.
Pancakes and fritters,
Say the bells of St. Peter's.
   Two sticks and an apple,
   Say the bells of Whitechapel.

Kettles and pans,
Say the bells of St Ann's,
   You owe me ten shillings,
   Say the bells of St Helen's.
     When will you pay me?
     Say the bells of Old Bailey.
When I grow rich,
Say the bells of Shoreditch.
Pray when will that be?
Say the bells of Stepney.
   I am sure I don't know,
   Says the great bell of Bow.

Anon

TERNARY OF LITTLES

Upon a Pipkin of Jelly given to a Lady

A LITTLE Saint best fits a little Shrine,
A little Prop best fits a little Vine,
As my small Cruse best fits my little Wine.

A little Seed best fits a little Soil,
A little Trade best fits a little Toil,
As my small Jar best fits my little Oil.

A little Bin best fits a little Bread,
A little Garland fits a little Head,
As my small Stuff best fits my little Shed.

A little Hearth best fits a little Fire,
A little Chapel fits a little Quire,
As my small Bell best fits my little Spire.

A little Stream best fits a little Boat,
A little Lead best fits a little Float,
As my small Pipe best fits my little Note.

A little Meat best fits a little Belly,
As sweetly, Lady, give me leave to tell Ye,
This little Pipkin fits this little Jelly.

Robert Herrick

FLEAS

GREAT fleas have little fleas upon their backs to bite 'em,
And little fleas have lesser fleas, and so *ad infinitum*.
And the great fleas themselves, in turn, have greater fleas to go on;
While these again have greater still, and greater still, and so on.

Augustus de Morgan

GHOULIES AND GHOSTIES

FROM ghoulies and ghosties and lang-legged beasties
And things that go bump in the night,
Good Lord, deliver us!

Traditional

TO EVERY THING
THERE IS A SEASON

Yesterday returneth not
Perchance tommorrow cometh not
There is today
misuse it not

THE SEVEN AGES

ALL the world's a stage,
And all the men and women merely players;
They have their exits and their entrances;
And one man in his time plays many parts,
His acts being seven ages. At first the infant,
Mewling and puking in the nurse's arms;
Then the whining school-boy, with his satchel
And shining morning face, creeping like snail
Unwillingly to school. And then the lover,
Sighing like furnace, with a woeful ballad
Made to his mistress' eyebrow. Then a soldier,
Full of strange oaths, and bearded like the pard,
Jealous in honour, sudden and quick in quarrel,
Seeking the bubble reputation
Even in the cannon's mouth. And then the justice,
In fair round belly with good capon lin'd,
With eyes severe and beard of formal cut,
Full of wise saws and modern instances;
And so he plays his part. The sixth age shifts
Into the lean and slipper'd pantaloon,
With spectacles on nose and pouch on side,
His youthful hose, well sav'd, a world too wide
For his shrunk shank; and his big manly voice,
Turning again towards childish treble, pipes
And whistles in his sound. Last scene of all,
That ends this strange eventful history,
Is second childishness and mere oblivion;
Sans teeth, sans eyes, sans taste, sans everything.

William Shakespeare, from As You Like It

GROWING UP

OUR birth is but a sleep and a forgetting:
The Soul that rises with us, our life's Star,
    Hath had elsewhere its setting,
        And cometh from afar:
    Not entirely in forgetfulness,
    And not in utter nakedness,
But trailing clouds of glory do we come
    From God, who is our home:
Heaven lies about us in our infancy!
Shades of the prison-house begin to close
    Upon the growing Boy.
But He beholds the light, and whence it flows,
    He sees it in his joy;
The Youth, who daily farther from the east
    Must travel, still is Nature's Priest,
    And by the vision splendid
    Is on his way attended;
At length the Man perceives it die away,
And fade into the light of common day.

William Wordsworth
Intimations of Immortality from Recollections of Early Childhood

A BOY'S SONG

WHERE the pools are bright and deep,
    Where the grey trout lies asleep,
Up the river and over the lea,
That's the way for Billy and me.

Where the blackbird sings the latest,
Where the hawthorn blooms the sweetest,
Where the nestlings chirp and flee,
That's the way for Billy and me.

Where the mowers mow the cleanest,
Where the hay lies thick and greenest,
There to track the homeward bee,
That's the way for Billy and me.

Where the hazel bank is steepest,
Where the shadow falls the deepest,

Where the clustering nuts fall free,
That's the way for Billy and me.

Why the boys should drive away
Little sweet maidens from their play,
Or love to banter and fight so well,
That's the thing I never could tell.

But this I know, I love to play
Through the meadow, among the hay;
Up the water and over the lea,
That's the way for Billy and me.

James Hogg

A BOAT AT NIGHT

ONE summer evening ...I found
A little boat tied to a willow tree
Within a rocky cave, its usual home.
Straight I unloosed her chain, and stepping in
Pushed from the shore. It was an act of stealth
And troubled pleasure, nor without the voice
Of mountain-echoes did my boat move on;
Leaving behind her still, on either side,
Small circles glittering idly in the moon,
Until they melted all into one track
Of sparkling light. But now, like one who rows,
Proud of his skill, to reach a chosen point
With an unswerving line, I fixed my view
Upon the summit of a craggy ridge,
The horizon's utmost boundary; for above
Was nothing but the stars and the grey sky.
She was an elfin pinnace; lustily
I dipped my oars into the silent lake,
And, as I rose upon the stroke, my boat
Went heaving through the water like a swan;
When, from behind that craggy steep till then
The horizon's bound, a huge peak, black and huge,
As if with voluntary power instinct
Upreared its head. I struck and struck again,
And growing still in stature the grim shape
Towered up between me and the stars, and still

For so it seemed, with purpose of its own
And measured motion like a living thing,
Strode after me. With trembling oars I turned,
And through the silent water stole my way
Back to the covert of the willow tree;
There in the mooring-place I left my bark,—
And through the meadows homeward went, in grave
And serious mood; but after I had seen
That spectacle, for many days, my brain
Worked with a dim and undetermined sense
Of unknown modes of being; o'er my thoughts
There hung a darkness, call it solitude
Or blank desertion. No familiar shapes
Remained, no pleasant images of trees,
Of sea or sky, no colours of green fields;
But huge and mighty forms, that do not live
Like living men, moved slowly through the mind
By day, and were a trouble to my dreams.

William Wordsworth, from
The Prelude—Childhood and School-time

THE TOYS

MY little son, who look'd from thoughtful eyes
And moved and spoke in quiet grown-up wise,
Having my law the seventh time disobey'd,
I struck him, and dismiss'd
With hard words and unkiss'd,
His Mother, who was patient, being dead.
Then, fearing lest his grief should hinder sleep,
I visited his bed,
But found him slumbering deep,
With darken'd eyelids and their lashes yet
From his late sobbing wet.
And I, with moan,
Kissing away his tears, left others of my own;
For, on a table drawn beside his head,
He had put, within his reach,
A box of counters and a red-vein'd stone,
A piece of glass abraded by the beach
And six or seven shells,

A bottle with bluebells
And two French copper coins, ranged there with careful art,
To comfort his sad heart.
So when that night I pray'd
To God, I wept and said:
Ah, when at last we lie with tranced breath,
Not vexing Thee in death,
And Thou rememberest of what toys
We made our joys,
How weakly understood,
Thy great commanded good,
Then, fatherly not less
Than I whom Thou hast moulded from the clay,
Thou'lt leave Thy wrath, and say,
'I will be sorry for their childishness.'

Coventry Patmore

THE LAND OF COUNTERPANE

WHEN I was sick and lay a-bed,
I had two pillows at my head,
And all my toys beside me lay,
To keep me happy all the day.

And sometimes for an hour or so,
I watched my leaden soldiers go,
With different uniforms and drills
Among the bedclothes, through the hills;

And sometimes sent my ships in fleets
All up and down among the sheets;
Or brought my trees and houses out,
And planted cities all about.

I was the giant great and still
That sits upon the pillow-hill,
And sees before him, dale and plain,
The pleasant land of counterpane.

Robert Louis Stevenson

THE SCHOOLMASTER

ABROAD WITH HIS SON

O WHAT harper could worthily harp it,
   Mine Edward! this wide-stretching wold
(Look out *wold*) with its wonderful carpet
   Of emerald, purple and gold!
Look well at it—also sharp, it
     Is getting cold.

The purple is heather (*erica*);
   The yellow, gorse—call'd sometime 'whin'.
Cruel boys on its prickles might spike a
   Green beetle as if on a pin.
You may roll in it, if you would like a
     Few holes in your skin.

You wouldn't? Then think how kind you
   Should be to insects who crave
Your compassion—and then, look behind you
   At yon barley-ears! Don't they look brave
As they undulate (*undulate*, mind you,
     From *unda, a wave*).

The noise of those sheep-bells, how faint it
   Sounds here—(on account of our height)!
And this hillock itself—who could paint it,
   With its changes of shadows and light?
Is it not—(never, Eddy, say 'ain't it')—
     A marvellous sight?

Then yon desolate eerie morasses,
   The haunts of the snipe and the hern—
(I shall question the two upper classes
   On *aquatiles*, when we return)—
Why, I see on them masses
     Of *filix* or fern.

How it interests e'en a beginner
   (Or tiro) like dear little Ned!
Is he listening? As I am a sinner,
   He's asleep—he is wagging his head.

WAKE UP! I'll go home to my dinner,
    And you to your bed.

The boundless ineffable prairie;
    The splendour of mountain and lake
With their hues that seem ever to vary;
    The mighty pine-forests which shake
In the wind, and in which the unwary
    May tread on a snake;

And this wold with its heathery garment
    Are themes undeniably great.
But—although there is not any harm in't—
    It's perhaps little good to dilate
On their charms to a dull little varmint
    Of seven or eight.

Charles Stuart Calverley

AT LORDS

IT is little I repair to the matches of the Southron folk,
  Though my own red roses there may blow;
It is little I repair to the matches of the Southron folk,
    Though the red roses crest the caps, I know.
For the field is full of shades as I near the shadowy coast,
And a ghostly batsman plays to the bowling of a ghost,
And I look through my tears on a soundless-clapping host
    As the run-stealers flicker to and fro,
        To and fro:—
  O my Hornby and my Barlow long ago!

Francis Thompson

LAVENDER'S BLUE

LAVENDER'S blue, dilly, dilly, lavender's green,
  When I am king, dilly, dilly, you shall be queen.
Who told you so, dilly, dilly, who told you so?
'Twas mine own heart, dilly, dilly, that told me so.

Call up your men, dilly, dilly, set them to work,
Some with a rake, dilly, dilly, some with a fork,
Some to make hay, dilly, dilly, some to thresh corn,
Whilst you and I, dilly, dilly, keep ourselves warm.   *Traditional*

AUNT TABITHA

WHATEVER I do, and whatever I say,
Aunt Tabitha tells me that isn't the way;
When *she* was a girl (forty summers ago)
Aunt Tabitha tells me they never did so.

Dear Aunt! If I only would take her advice!
But I like my own way, and I find it *so* nice!
And besides, I forget half the things I am told;
But they all will come back to me—when I am old.

If a youth passes by, it may happen, no doubt,
He may chance to look in as I chance to look out;
She would never endure an impertinent stare—
It is *horrid*, she says, and I mustn't sit there.

A walk in the moonlight has pleasures, I own,
But it isn't quite safe to be walking alone;
So I take a lad's arm— just for safety, you know—
But Aunt Tabitha tells me *they* didn't do so.

How wicked we are, and how good they were then!
They kept at arm's length those detestable men;
What an era of virtue she lived in!—But stay—
Were the *men* all such rogues in Aunt Tabitha's day?

If the men *were* so wicked, I'll ask my papa
How he dared to propose to my darling mamma?
Was he like the rest of them? Goodness! Who knows?
And what shall *I* say, if a wretch should propose?

I am thinking if aunt knew so little of sin,
What a wonder Aunt Tabitha's aunt must have been!
And her grand-aunt—it scares me—how shockingly sad
That we girls of today are so frightfully bad!

A martyr will save us, and nothing else can;
Let *me* perish—to rescue some wretched young man!
Though when to the altar a victim I go,
Aunt Tabitha 'll tell me *she* never did so!

Oliver Wendell Holmes

GREENSLEEVES

ALAS, my love, you do me wrong
To cast me off so discourteously,
And I have loved you so long,
   Delighting in your company.

> *Greensleeves was all my joy,*
> *Greensleeves was my delight,*
> *Greensleeves was my heart of gold,—*
> *And who but my lady Greensleeves.*

I have been ready at your hand
   To grant whatever you would crave;
I have both wagered life and land,
   Your love and goodwill for to have. *(chorus)*

Thou couldst desire no earthly thing,
   But still thou hadst it readily;
Thy music still to play and sing,
   And yet thou wouldst not love me. *(chorus)*

Well, I will pray to God on high
   That thou constancy mayest see,
And that yet once before I die,
   Thou will vouchsafe to love me. *(chorus)*.

Traditional

THE BARGAIN

MY true love hath my heart, and I have his,
By just exchange one for another given:
I hold his dear, and mine he cannot miss,
   There never was a better bargain driven:
     My true love hath my heart, and I have his.

His heart in me keeps him and me in one,
   My heart in him his thoughts and senses guides:
He loves my heart, for once it was his own,
   I cherish his because in me it bides:
     My true love hath my heart, and I have his.

Sir Philip Sidney

O MISTRESS MINE

O MISTRESS mine, where are you roaming?
O stay and hear; your true love's coming,
That can sing both high and low.
  Trip no further, pretty sweeting;
Journeys end in lovers meeting,
  Every wise man's son doth know.

What is love? 'Tis not hereafter;
  Present mirth hath present laughter;
What's to come is still unsure.
  In delay there lies no plenty,
Then come kiss me, sweet and twenty,
  Youth's a stuff will not endure.

William Shakespeare, from Twelfth Night

SONG TO CELIA

DRINK to me only with thine eyes,
  And I will pledge with mine;
Or leave a kiss but in the cup
  And I'll not look for wine.
The thirst that from the soul doth rise,
  Doth ask a drink divine;
But might I of Jove's Nectar sup,
  I would not change for thine.

I sent thee late a rosy wreath,
  Not so much honouring thee
As giving it a hope that there
  It could not wither'd be;
But thou thereon didst only breathe,
  And sent'st it back to me;
Since when it grows, and smells, I swear,
  Not of itself but thee!

Ben Jonson

SONG FOR A GIRL

FROM 'LOVE TRIUMPHANT'

YOUNG I am, and yet unskill'd
How to make a Lover yield:
How to keep, or how to gain,
When to love; and when to feign.

Take me, take me, some of you,
While I yet am Young and True;
Ere I can my Soul disguise;
Heave my Breasts, and roll my Eyes.

Stay not till I learn the way,
How to Lie, and to Betray:
He that has me first, is blest,
For I may deceive the rest.

Cou'd I find a blooming Youth,
Full of Love, and full of Truth,
Brisk, and of a jaunty mean
I shou'd long to be Fifteen.

John Dryden

JENNY KISS'D ME

JENNY kiss'd me when we met,
Jumping from the chair she sat in;
  Time, you thief, who love to get
  Sweets into your list, put that in!
Say I'm weary, say I'm sad,
  Say that health and wealth have miss'd me,
Say I'm growing old, but add,
  Jenny kiss'd me.

James Henry Leigh Hunt

A RED, RED ROSE

O MY Luve's like a red, red rose
That's newly sprung in June:
O my Luve's like the melodie
  That's sweetly play'd in tune!

So fair art thou, my bonnie lass,
    So deep in luve am I:
And I will luve thee still, my dear,
    Till a' the seas gang dry:

Till a' the seas gang dry, my dear,
    And the rocks melt wi' the sun;
I will luve thee still, my dear,
    While the sands o' life shall run.

And fare thee weel, my only Luve,
    And fare thee weel a while!
And I will come again, my Luve,
    Tho' it were ten thousand mile.

Robert Burns

SHE WALKS IN BEAUTY

SHE walks in beauty, like the night
Of cloudless climes and starry skies;
And all that's best of dark and bright
    Meet in her aspect and her eyes:
Thus mellow'd to that tender light
    Which heaven to gaudy day denies.

One shade the more, one ray the less,
    Had half impair'd the nameless grace
Which waves in every raven tress,
    Or softly lightens o'er her face;
Where thoughts serenely sweet express
    How pure, how dear their dwelling-place.

And on that cheek, and o'er that brow,
    So soft, so calm, yet eloquent,
The smiles that win, the tints that glow,
    But tell of days in goodness spent,
A mind at peace with all below,
    A heart whose love is innocent!

George Gordon, Lord Byron

PERSICOS ODI

DEAR Lucy, you know what my wish is,—
I hate all your Frenchified fuss:
Your silly *entrées* and made dishes
    Were never intended for us.
No footman in lace and in ruffles
    Need dangle behind my arm-chair;
And never mind seeking for truffles,
    Although they be ever so rare.

But a plain leg of mutton, my Lucy,
    I pr'ythee get ready at three:
Have it smoking, and tender, and juicy,
    And what better meat can there be?
And when it has feasted the master,
    'Twill amply suffice for the maid;
Meanwhile I will smoke my canaster,
And tipple my ale in the shade.

William Thackeray

YOUNG LOCHINVAR

O YOUNG Lochinvar is come out of the west,
Through all the wide Border his steed was the best;
And save his good broadsword he weapons had none,
He rode all unarm'd, and he rode all alone.
So faithful in love, and so dauntless in war,
There never was knight like the young Lochinvar.

He staid not for brake and he stopp'd not for stone,
He swam the Eske river where ford there was none;
But ere he alighted at Netherby gate,
The bride had consented, the gallant came late:
For a laggard in love, and a dastard in war,
Was to wed the fair Ellen of brave Lochinvar.

So bravely he enter'd the Netherby Hall,
Among bride's-men, and kinsmen, and brothers and all:
Then spake the bride's father, his hand on his sword,
(For the poor craven bridgroom said never a word),
'O come ye in peace here, or come ye in war,
Or to dance at our bridal, young Lord Lochinvar?'

'I long woo'd your daughter, my suit you denied;—
Love swells like the Solway, but ebbs like its tide—
And now I am come, with this lost love of mine,
To lead but one measure, drink one cup of wine.
There are maidens in Scotland more lovely by far,
That would gladly be bride to the young Lochinvar.'

The bride kiss'd the goblet: the knight took it up,
He quaffed off the wine, and he threw down the cup.
She look'd down to blush, and she look'd up to sigh,
With a smile on her lips, and a tear in her eye.
He took her soft hand, ere her mother could bar,—
'Now tread we a measure!' said young Lochinvar.

So stately his form, and so lovely her face,
That never a hall such a galliard did grace;
While her mother did fret, and her father did fume,
And the bridegroom stood dangling his bonnet and plume;
And the bride-maidens whisper'd, ''Twere better by far,
To have match'd our fair cousin with young Lochinvar.'

One touch to her hand, and one word in her ear,
When they reach'd the hall-door, and the charger stood near;
So light to the croupe the fair lady he swung,
So light to the saddle before her he sprung!
'She is won! we are gone, over bank, bush and scaur;
They'll have fleet steeds that follow,' quoth young Lochinvar.

There was mounting 'mong Graemes of the Netherby clan;
Forsters, Fenwicks, and Musgraves, they rode and they ran:
There was racing and chasing on Cannobie Lee,
But the lost bride of Netherby ne'er did they see.
So daring in love, and so dauntless in war,
Have you e'er heard of gallant like young Lochinvar?

Sir Walter Scott, a ballad from Marmion

MY LAST DUCHESS

FERRARA

THAT'S my last Duchess painted on the wall,
Looking as if she were alive. I call
That piece a wonder, now: Frà Pandolf's hands
Worked busily a day, and there she stands.
Will't please you sit and look at her? I said
'Frà Pandolf' by design, for never read
Strangers like you that pictured countenance,
The depth and passion of its earnest glance,
But to myself they turned (since none puts by
The curtain I have drawn for you, but I)
And seemed as they would ask me, if they durst,
How such a glance came there; so, not the first
Are you to turn and ask thus. Sir, 'twas not
Her husband's presence only, called that spot
Of joy into the Duchess' cheek: perhaps
Frà Pandolf chanced to say 'Her mantle laps
Over my lady's wrist too much,' or 'Paint
Must never hope to reproduce the faint
Half-flush that dies along her throat:' such stuff
Was courtesy, she thought, and cause enough
For calling up that spot of joy. She had
A heart—how shall I say?—too soon made glad,
Too easily impressed; she liked whate'er
She looked on, and her looks went everywhere.
Sir, 'twas all one! My favour at her breast,
The dropping of the daylight in the West,
The bough of cherries some officious fool
Broke in the orchard for her, the white mule
She rode with round the terrace—all and each
Would draw from her alike the approving speech,
Or blush, at least. She thanked men,—good! but thanked
Somehow—I know not how—as if she ranked
My gift of a nine-hundred-years-old name
With anybody's gift. Who'd stoop to blame
This sort of trifling? Even had you skill
In speech—(which I have not)—to make your will
Quite clear to such an one, and say, 'Just this
Or that in you disgusts me; here you miss,

Or there exceed the mark'—and if she let
Herself be lessoned so, nor plainly set
Her wits to yours, forsooth, and made excuse,
—E'en then would be some stooping; and I choose
Never to stoop. Oh sir, she smiled, no doubt,
Whene'er I passed her; but who passed without
Much the same smile? This grew; I gave commands;
Then all smiles stopped together. There she stands
As if alive. Will't please you rise? We'll meet
The company below, then. I repeat,
The Count your master's known munificence
Is ample warrant that no just pretence
Of mine for dowry will be disallowed;
Though his fair daughter's self, as I avowed
At starting, is my object. Nay, we'll go
Together down, sir. Notice Neptune, though,
Taming a sea-horse, thought a rarity,
Which Claus of Innsbruck cast in bronze for me!

Robert Browning

MEETING AT NIGHT

THE grey sea and the long black land;
And the yellow half-moon large and low;
And the startled little waves that leap
In fiery ringlets from their sleep,
As I gain the cove with pushing prow,
And quench its speed i' the slushy sand.

Then a mile of warm sea-scented beach;
Three fields to cross till a farm appears;
A tap at the pane, the quick sharp scratch
And blue spurt of a lighted match,
And a voice less loud, thro' its joys and fears,
Than two hearts beating each to each!

Robert Browning

PARTING AT MORNING

ROUND the cape of a sudden came the sea,
And the sun look'd over the mountain's rim:
And straight was a path of gold for him,
And the need of a world of men for me.

Robert Browning

WOMAN

WHEN lovely Woman stoops to folly,
   And finds too late that men betray,
What charm can soothe her melancholy?
   What art can wash her guilt away?

The only art her guilt to cover,
   To hide her shame from every eye,
To give repentance to her lover,
   And wring his bosom, is—to die.

Oliver Goldsmith, Song from the Vicar of Wakefield

WE'LL GO NO MORE A-ROVING

SO, we'll go no more a-roving
   So late into the night,
Though the heart be still as loving,
   And the moon be still as bright.

For the sword outwears its sheath,
   And the soul wears out the breast,
And the heart must pause to breathe,
   And love itself have rest.

Though the night was made for loving,
   And the day returns too soon,
Yet we'll go no more a-roving
   By the light of the moon.

George Gordon, Lord Byron

AULD LANG SYNE

SHOULD auld acquaintance be forgot,
And never brought to min'?
Should auld acquaintance be forgot,
   And days o' lang syne?

> *For auld lang syne, my dear,*
>   *For auld lang syne,*
> *We'll tak a cup o' kindness yet*
>   *For auld lang syne.*

We twa hae rin about the braes,
   And pu'd the gowans fine;
But we've wander'd monie a weary fit
   Sin' auld lang syne. *(chorus)*

We twa hae paidl't i' the burn,
   Frae mornin' sun till dine;
But seas between us braid hae roar'd
   Sin' auld lang syne. *(chorus)*

And here's a hand, my trusty fiere,
   And gie's a hand o' thine;
And we'll tak a right guid-willie waught
   For auld land syne. *(chorus)*

And surely ye'll be your pint-stowp,
   And surely I'll be mine;
And we'll tak a cup o' kindness yet
   For auld lang syne. *(chorus)*

Robert Burns

FESTE'S SONG

COME away, come away, death;
   And in sad cypress let me be laid;
   Fly away, fly away, breath,
I am slain by a fair cruel maid.
My shroud of white, stuck all with yew,
      O, prepare it!
My part of death no one so true
      Did share it.

TO EVERY THING THERE IS A SEASON

    Not a flower, not a flower sweet,
On my black coffin let there be strown;
    Not a friend, not a friend greet
My poor corpse where my bones shall be thrown;
A thousand thousand sighs to save,
        Lay me, O, where
Sad true lover never finds my grave,
        To weep there!

William Shakespeare, from Twelfth Night

DEATH

DEATH be not proud, though some have called thee
Mighty and dreadful, for, thou art not so:
For those whom thou think'st, thou dost overthrow
Die not, poor Death; nor yet canst thou kill me.
From Rest and Sleep, which but thy picture be,
Much pleasure, then from thee much more must flow;
And soonest our best men with thee do go—
Rest of their bones, and soul's delivery!
Thou'rt slave to fate, chance, kings, and desperate men,
And dost with poison, war, and sickness dwell;
And poppy, or charms can make us sleep as well
And better than thy stroke. Why swellest thou then?
One short sleep past, we wake eternally,
And death shall be no more: Death, thou shalt die!

John Donne from The Divine Poems

REQUIEM

UNDER the wide and starry sky
    Dig the grave and let me lie:
Glad did I live and gladly die,
    And I laid me down with a will.

This be the verse you grave for me:
    Here he lies where he long'd to be;
Home is the sailor, home from the sea,
    And the hunter home from the hill.

Robert Louis Stevenson

THE SONG OF GUIDERIUS AND ARVIRAGUS

FEAR no more the heat o' th' sun
Nor the furious winter's rages;
Thou thy worldly task hast done,
　　Home art gone, and ta'en thy wages.
Golden lads and girls all must,
As chimney-sweepers, come to dust.

Fear no more the frown o' th' great;
　　Thou art past the tyrant's stroke.
Care no more to clothe and eat;
　　To thee the reed is as the oak.
The sceptre, learning, physic, must
All follow this and come to dust.

Fear no more the lightning flash,
　　Nor th' all-dreaded thunder-stone;
Fear not slander, censure rash;
　　Thou hast finish'd joy and moan.
All lovers young, all lovers must
Consign to thee and come to dust.

William Shakespeare, from Cymbeline

A PEACOCK
WITH A FIERY TAIL

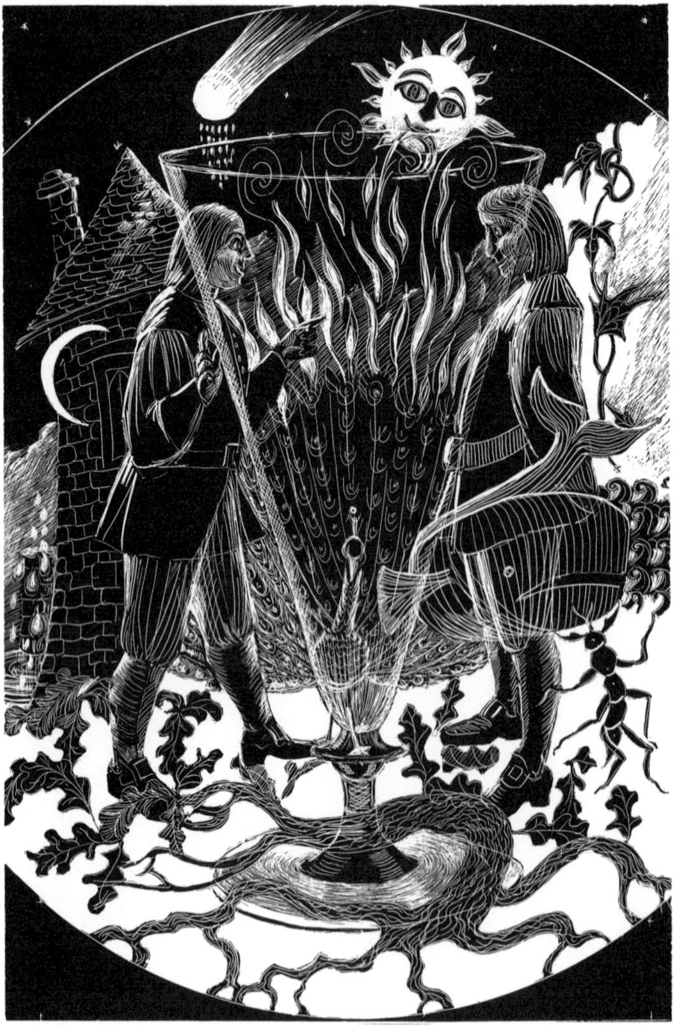

A PEACOCK WITH A FIERY TAIL

I SAW a peacock with a fiery tail,
I saw a blazing comet drop down hail,
I saw a cloud wrapped with ivy round,
I saw an oak creep upon the ground,
I saw a pismire swallow up a whale,
I saw the sea brimful of ale.
I saw a Venice glass five fathom deep,
I saw a well full of men's tears that weep,
I saw red eyes all of a flaming fire,
I saw a house bigger than the moon and higher.
I saw the sun at twelve o'clock at night;
I saw the man that saw this wondrous sight.

Anon: from the Westminster Drollery, 1671

THE LION AND THE UNICORN

THE lion and the unicorn
   Were fighting for the crown:
The lion beat the unicorn
   All round the town.
Some gave them white bread,
   Some gave them brown;
Some gave them plum cake,
   And sent them out of town.

Traditional

TWINKLE, TWINKLE, LITTLE BAT!

TWINKLE, twinkle, little bat!
   How I wonder what you're at!
Up above the world you fly,
Like a tea-tray in the sky.

Lewis Carroll, from Alice in Wonderland

IF ALL THE WORLD WERE PAPER

IF all the world were paper,
And all the sea were ink,
And all the trees were bread and cheese,
   What should we do for drink?

If all the world were sand-o,
  Oh, then what should we lack-o?
If, as they say, there were no clay,
  How should we take tobacco?

If all our vessels ran-a,
  If none but had a crack,
If Spanish apes ate all the grapes,
  How should we do for sack?

If friars had no bald pates,
  Nor nuns had no dark cloisters;
If all the seas were beans and peas,
  How should we do for oysters?

If all things were eternal,
  And nothing their end bringing;
If this should be, then how should we
  Here make an end of singing?

Anon

THE GREAT PANJANDRUM

SO she went into the garden
To cut a cabbage leaf
To make an apple-pie;
And at the same time
A great she-bear, coming down the street,
Pops his head into the shop.
'What! No soap?'
  So he died,
And she very imprudently married the Barber.
And there were present
  the Picninnies,
    the Joblillies,
      and the Garyulies,
And the great Panjandrum himself,
With the little round button on top;
And they all fell to playing the game of catch-as-catch-can,
Till the gunpowder ran out at the heels of their boots.

Samuel Foote

JABBERWOCKY

'TWAS brillig, and the slithy toves
    Did gyre and gimble in the wabe;
All mimsy were the borogroves,
    And the mome raths outgrabe.

'Beware the Jabberwock, my son!
    The jaws that bite, the claws that catch!
Beware the Jubjub bird, and shun
    The frumious Bandersnatch!'

He took his vorpal sword in hand:
    Long time the manxome foe he sought—
So rested he by the Tumtum tree,
    And stood awhile in thought.

And as in uffish thought he stood,
    The Jabberwock, with eyes of flame,
Came whiffling through the tulgey wood,
    And burbled as it came!

One, two! One, two! And through and through
    The vorpal sword went snicker-snack!
He left it dead, and with its head
    He went galumphing back.

'And hast thou slain the Jabberwock?
    Come to my arms, my beamish boy!
O frabjous day! Callooh! Callay!'
    He chortled in his joy.

Lewis Carroll, from Through the Looking-glass

A SHIP A-SAILING

I SAW a ship a-sailing,
    A-sailing on the sea,
And oh! it was all laden
    With pretty things for thee!

There were comfits in the cabin,
    And apples in the hold;
The sails were made of silk,
    And the masts were made of gold.

The four-and-twenty sailors
 That stood between the decks,
Were four-and-twenty white mice,
 With chains about their necks.

The captain was a duck,
 With a packet on his back;
And when the ship began to move,
 The captain said: 'Quack! quack!'

Anon

THE LOBSTER QUADRILLE

'WILL you walk a little faster?' said a whiting to a snail,
 "There's a porpoise close behind us, and he's treading on my tail.
See how eagerly the lobsters and the turtles all advance!
They are waiting on the shingle—will you come and join the dance?
 Will you, won't you, will you, won't you,
  Will you join the dance?
 Will you, won't you, will you, won't you,
  Won't you join the dance?'

'You can really have no notion how delightful it will be,
When they take us up and throw us, with the lobsters, out to sea!'
But the snail replied 'Too far, too far!' and gave a look askance—
Said he thanked the whiting kindly, but he would not join the dance.
 Would not, could not, would not, could not,
  Would not join the dance.
 Would not, could not, would not, could not,
  Could not join the dance.

'What matters it how far we go?' his scaly friend replied.
'There is another shore, you know, upon the other side.
The farther off from England the nearer is to France—
Then turn not pale, beloved snail, but come and join the dance.
 Will you, won't you, will you, won't you,
  Will you join the dance?
 Will you, won't you, will you, won't you,
  Won't you join the dance?'

Lewis Carroll, from Alice in Wonderland

MY LITTLE NUT-TREE

I HAD a little nut-tree, nothing would it bear
But a silver nutmeg and a golden pear;
The King of Spain's daughter came to visit me,
And all was because of my little nut-tree.
I skipped over water, I danced over sea,
And all the birds in the air couldn't catch me.

Anon

CALICO PIE

CALICO Pie,
The little Birds fly
Down to the calico tree,
   Their wings were blue,
   And they sang 'Tilly-loo!'
Till away they flew—
     And they never came back to me!
       They never came back!
       They never came back!
     They never came back to me!

Calico Jam,
   The little Fish swam,
Over the syllabub sea,
   He took off his hat,
   To the Sole and the Sprat,
   And the Willeby-wat,—
     But he never came back to me!
       He never came back!
       He never came back!
     He never came back to me!

Calico Ban,
   The little Mice ran,
To be ready in time for tea,
   Flippity flup,
   They drank it all up,
   And danced in the cup,—
     But they never came back to me!
       They never came back!

>   They never came back!
>   They never came back to me!

Calico Drum,
  The Grasshoppers come,
The Butterfly, Beetle, and Bee,
  Over the ground,
  Around and around,
  With a hop and a bound,—
    But they never came back!
    They never came back!
    They never came back!
    They never came back to me!

Edward Lear

THE MAD GARDENER'S SONG

HE thought he saw an Elephant,
  That practised on a fife:
He looked again, and found it was
  A letter from his wife.
'At length I realize' he said,
  'The bitterness of Life!'

He thought he saw a Buffalo
  Upon the chimney-piece:
He looked again, and found it was
  His Sister's Husband's Niece.
'Unless you leave this house,' he said,
  'I'll send for the police!'

He thought he saw a Rattlesnake
  That questioned him in Greek:
He looked again, and found it was
  The Middle of Next Week.
'The one thing I regret,' he said,
  'Is that it cannot speak!'

He thought he saw a Banker's Clerk
  Descending from a 'bus:
He looked again, and found it was
  A Hippopotamus.

'If this should stay to dine,' he said,
  'There won't be much for us!'

He thought he saw a Kangaroo
  That worked a coffee-mill:
He looked again, and found it was
  A Vegetable-Pill.
'Were I to swallow this,' he said,
  'I would be very ill!'

He thought he saw a Coach-and-Four
  That stood beside his bed:
He looked again, and found it was
  A Bear without a Head:
'Poor thing,' he said, 'poor silly thing!
  It's waiting to be fed!'

He thought he saw an Albatross
  That fluttered round the lamp:
He looked again, and found it was
  A penny Postage Stamp.
'You'd best be getting home,' he said,
  'The nights are very damp.'

He thought he saw a Garden-Door
  That opened with a key:
He looked again, and found it was
  A Double Rule of Three:
'And all its mystery,' he said,
  'Is clear as day to me!'

He thought he saw an Argument
  That proved he was the Pope:
He looked again, and found it was
  A bar of Mottled Soap.
'A fact so dread,' he faintly said,
  'Extinguishes all hope!'

Lewis Carroll

THE CUMMERBUND

AN INDIAN POEM

SHE sate upon her Dobie
  To watch the Evening Star,
And all the Punkahs as they passed
  Cried: 'My! how fair you are!'
Around her bower, with quivering leaves
  The tall Kumsamahs grew,
And Kitmutgars in wild festoons
  Hung down from Tchokis blue.

Below her home the river rolled
  With soft meloobious sound,
Where golden-finned Chuprassies swam,
  In myriads circling round.
Above, on tallest trees remote,
  Green Ayahs perched alone,
And all night long the Mussak moan'd
  Its melancholy tone.

And where the purple Nullahs threw
  Their branches far and wide—
And silvery Goreewallahs flew
  In silence, side by side—
The little Bheesties' twittering cry
  Rose on the fragrant air,
And oft the angry Jampan howled
  Deep in his hateful lair.

She sate upon her Dobie—
  She heard the Nimmak hum—
When all at once a cry arose:
  'The Cummerbund is come!'
In vain she fled;—with open jaws
  The angry monster followed,
And so (before assistance came),
  That Lady Fair was swallowed.

They sought in vain for even a bone
  Respectfully to bury—
They said: 'Hers was a dreadful fate!'
  (And Echo answered 'Very.')

They nailed her Dobie to the wall,
  Where last her form was seen,
And underneath they wrote these words,
  In yellow, blue and green:

Beware, ye Fair! Ye Fair, beware!
  Nor sit out late at night—
Lest horrid Cummerbunds should come,
  And swallow you outright.

Edward Lear

THE OWL AND THE PUSSY-CAT

THE Owl and the Pussy-Cat went to sea
  In a beautiful pea-green boat.
They took some honey, and plenty of money,
  Wrapped up in a five-pound note.
The Owl looked up to the stars above,
  And sang to a small guitar,
'O lovely Pussy! O Pussy, my love,
  What a beautiful Pussy you are,
      You are,
      You are!
  What a beautiful pussy you are!'

Pussy said to the Owl, 'You elegant fowl!
  How charmingly sweet you sing!
O let us be married! too long we have tarried:
  But what shall we do for a ring?'
They sailed away, for a year and a day,
  To the land where the Bong-Tree grows,
And there in a wood a Piggy-Wig stood,
  With a ring on the end of his nose,
      His nose,
      His nose,
  With a ring on the end of his nose.

'Dear Pig, are you willing to sell for one shilling
  Your ring?' said the Piggy, 'I will.'
So they took it away, and were married next day
  By the Turkey who lives on the hill.
They dined on mince, and slices of quince,

Which they ate with a runcible spoon;
And hand in hand, on the edge of the sand,
　　They danced by the light of the moon,
　　　　The moon,
　　　　The moon,
They danced by the light of the moon.

Edward Lear

A-SITTING ON A GATE

'I'LL tell thee everything I can;
　　There's little to relate.
I saw an aged aged man
　　A-sitting on a gate.
'Who are you, aged man?' I said,
　　'And how is it you live?'
And his answer trickled through my head
　　Like water through a sieve.

He said, 'I look for butterflies
　　That sleep among the wheat:
I make them into mutton pies,
　　And sell them in the street.
I sell them unto men,' he said,
　　'Who sail the stormy seas;
And that's the way I get my bread—
　　A trifle, if you please.'

But I was thinking of a plan
　　To dye one's whiskers green,
And always use so large a fan
　　That they could not be seen.
So, having no reply to give
　　To what the old man said,
I cried, 'Come, tell my how you live!'
　　And thumped him on the head,

His accents mild took up the tale:
　　He said 'I go my ways,
And when I find a mountain-rill,
　　I set it in a blaze;
And thence they make a stuff they call

Rowland's Macassar Oil—
Yet twopence-halfpenny is all
 They give me for my toil.'

But I was thinking of a way
 To feed oneself on batter,
And so go on from day to day
 Getting a little fatter.
I shook him well from side to side,
 Until his face was blue:
'Come, tell me how you live,' I cried
 'And what it is you do!'

He said, 'I hunt for haddocks' eyes
 Among the heather bright,
And work them into waistcoat-buttons
 In the silent night.
And these I do not sell for gold
 Or coin of silvery shine,
But for a copper halfpenny,
 And that will purchase nine.

I sometimes dig for buttered rolls,
 Or set limed twigs for crabs;
I sometimes search the grassy knolls
 For wheels of Hansome-cabs.
And that's the way' (he gave a wink)
 'By which I get my wealth—
And very gladly will I drink
 Your Honour's noble health.'

I heard him then, for I had just
 Completed my design
To keep the Menai bridge from rust
 By boiling it in wine.
I thanked him much for telling me
 The way he got his wealth,
But chiefly for his wish that he
 Might drink my noble health.

And now, if e'er by chance I put
 My fingers into glue,
Or madly squeeze a right-hand foot

    Into a left-hand shoe,
Or if I drop upon my toe
    A very heavy weight,
I weep, for it reminds me so
Of that old man I used to know—
Whose look was mild, whose speech was slow
Whose hair was whiter than the snow,
Whose face was very like a crow,
With eyes, like cinders, all aglow,
Who seemed distracted with his woe,
Who rocked his body to and fro,
And muttered mumblingly and low,
As if his mouth were full of dough,
Who snorted like a buffalo—
That summer evening long ago
    A-sitting on a gate.

Lewis Carroll, from Through the Looking-glass

NIGHT AND DAY, BOTH SWEET THINGS

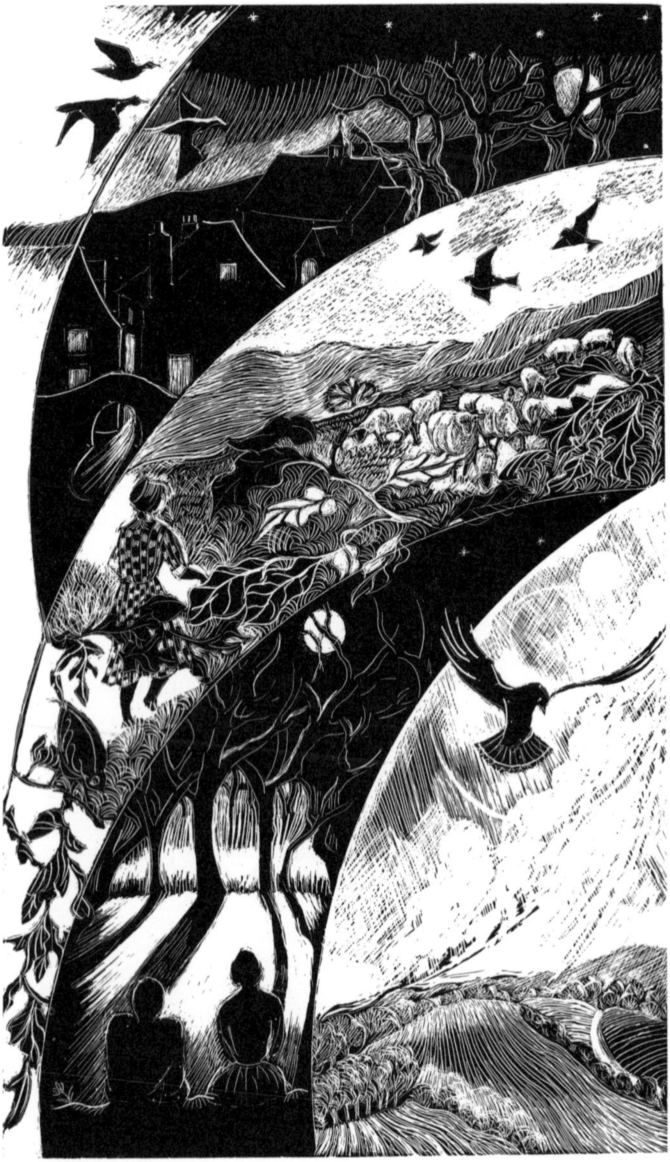

DAWN

BUT look, the morn, in russet mantle clad,
Walks o'er the dew of yon high eastward hill.

William Shakespeare, from Hamlet

PIPPA'S SONG

THE year's at the spring
And day's at the morn;
Morning's at seven;
The hill-side's dew-pearled;
The lark's on the wing;
The snail's on the thorn:
God's in his heaven—
All's right with the world!

Robert Browning, Song from Pippa Passes

THE WINDHOVER

TO CHRIST OUR LORD

I CAUGHT this morning morning's minion, king-
dom of daylight's dauphin, dapple-dawn-drawn Falcon, in his riding
   Of the rolling level underneath him steady air, and striding
High there, how he rung upon the rein of a wimpling wing
In his ecstasy! then off, off forth on swing,
   As a skate's heel sweeps smooth on a bow-bend: the hurl and gliding
   Rebuffed the big wind. My heart in hiding
Stirred for a bird,—the achieve of, the mastery of the thing!

Brute beauty and valour and act, oh, air, pride, plume here
   Buckle! AND the fire that breaks from thee then, a billion
Times told lovelier, more dangerous, O my chevalier!

   No wonder of it: shéer plód makes plough down sillion
Shine, and blue-black embers, ah my dear,
   Fall, gall themselves, and gash gold-vermilion.

Gerard Manley Hopkins

SONNET THIRTY-THREE

FULL many a glorious morning have I seen
Flatter the mountain-tops with sovereign eye,
Kissing with golden face the meadows green,
Gilding pale streams with heavenly alchemy;
Anon permit the basest clouds to ride
With ugly rack on his celestial face,
And from the forlorn world his visage hide,
Stealing unseen to west with this disgrace.
Even so my sun one early morn did shine
With all triumphant splendour on my brow;
But out, alack! he was but one hour mine,
The region cloud hath mask'd him from me now.
    Yet him for this my love no whit disdaineth;
    Suns of the world may stain when heaven's sun staineth.

William Shakespeare

THE COMING OF DAY

TO hear the lark begin his flight,
And, singing, startle the dull night,
From his watch-tower in the skies,
Till the dappled dawn doth rise;
Then to come, in spite of sorrow,
And at my window bid good-morrow,
Through the sweet-briar or the vine,
Or the twisted eglantine;
While the cock, with lively din,
Scatters the rear of darkness thin,
And to the stack, or the barn door,
Stoutly struts his dames before:
Oft listening how the hounds and horn
Cheerly rouse the slumbering morn,
From the side of some hoar hill,
Through the high wood echoing shrill:
Sometime walking, not unseen,
By hedge row elms, on hillocks green,
Right against the eastern gate
Where the great Sun begins his state,
Robed in flames and amber light,
The clouds in thousand liveries dight;

NIGHT AND DAY, BOTH SWEET THINGS

While the ploughman, near at hand,
Whistles o'er the furrowed land,
And the milkmaid singeth blithe,
And the mower whets his scythe,
And every shepherd tells his tale
Under the hawthorn in the dale.

John Milton, from L'Allegro

THE ANGELUS

AVE MARIA! o'er the earth and sea,
That heavenliest hour of Heaven is worthiest thee!

Ave Maria! blessed be the hour!
   The time, the clime, the spot, where I so oft
Have felt a moment in its fullest power
   Sink o'er the earth so beautiful and soft,
While swung the deep bell in the distant tower,
   Or the faint dying day-hymn stole aloft,
And not a breath crept through the rosy air,
And yet the forest leaves seem'd stirr'd with prayer.

Ave Maria! 'tis the hour of prayer!
   Ave Maria! 'tis the hour of love!
Ave Maria! may our spirits dare
   Look up to thine and to thy Son's above!
Ave Maria! oh that face so fair!
   Those downcast eyes beneath the Almighty dove—
What though 'tis but a pictured image?—strike,
That painting is no idol,—'tis too like.

George Gordon, Lord Byron, from Don Juan

STAR LIGHT, STAR BRIGHT

Star light, star bright,
First star I see tonight.
I wish I could, I wish I might
   Have the wish I wish tonight.

Traditional

STILLNESS

WHEN the words rustle no more,
    And the last work's done,
When the bolt lies deep in the door,
    And Fire, our Sun,
Falls on the dark-laned meadows of the floor;

When from the clock's last chime to the next chime
    Silence beats his drum,
And Space with gaunt grey eyes and her brother Time
    Wheeling and whispering come,
She with the mould of form, and he with the loom of rhyme:

Then twittering out in the night my thought-birds flee,
    I am emptied of all my dreams:
I only hear Earth turning, only see
    Ether's long bankless streams,
And only know I should drown if you laid not your hand on me.

James Elroy Flecker

BEFORE SLEEPING

MATTHEW, Mark, Luke and John,
The bed be blest that I lie on.
Before I lay me down to sleep
I give my soul to Christ to keep.
Four corners to my bed
Four angels there a-spread,
Two to foot, and two to head,
And four to carry me when I'm dead.
I go by sea, I go by land,
The Lord made me with His right hand.
If any danger come to me,
Sweet Jesus Christ, deliver me.
He's the branch and I'm the flower,
May God send me a happy hour;
And if I die before I wake,
I pray that Christ my soul will take.

Thomas Ady, and Traditional

THE NIGHT HAS A THOUSAND EYES

THE night has a thousand eyes,
  And the day but one;
Yet the light of the bright world dies
  With the dying sun.

The mind has a thousand eyes,
  And the heart but one;
Yet the light of a whole life dies
  When love is done.

Francis William Bourdillon

AT NIGHT

HOME, home from the horizon far and clear,
  Hither the soft wings sweep;
Flocks of memories of the day draw near
  The dovecote doors of sleep.

Oh, which are they that come through sweetest light
    Of all these homing birds?
Which with the straightest and swiftest flight?
    Your words to me, your words!

Alice Meynell

MOONLIGHT AT BELMONT

HOW sweet the moonlight sleeps upon this bank!
Here will we sit and let the sounds of music
Creep in our ears; soft stillness and the night
Become the touches of sweet harmony.
Sit, Jessica. Look how the floor of heaven
Is thick inlaid with patines of bright gold;
There's not the smallest orb which thou behold'st
But in his motion like an angel sings,
Still quiring to the young-ey'd cherubins;
Such harmony is in immortal souls,
But whilst this muddy vesture of decay
Doth grossly close it in, we cannot hear it.

William Shakespeare, from The Merchant of Venice

THE LAND OF NOD

FROM breakfast on through all the day
At home among my friends I stay,
But every night I go abroad
Afar into the Land of Nod.

All by myself I have to go,
With none to tell me what to do—
All alone beside the streams
And up the mountain-sides of dreams.

The strangest things are there for me,
Both things to eat and things to see,
And many frightening things abroad,
Till morning in the Land of Nod.

Try as I like to find my way,
I never can get back by day,
Nor can remember plain and clear
The curious music that I hear.

Robert Louis Stevenson

GOLDEN SLUMBERS

GOLDEN slumbers kiss your eyes,
Smiles awake you when you rise.
Sleep, pretty wantons, do not cry,
    And I will sing a lullaby:
Rock them, rock them, lullaby.

Care is heavy, therefore sleep you,
    You are care, and care must keep you.
Sleep, pretty wantons, do not cry,
    And I will sing a lullaby:
Rock them, rock them, lullaby.

Thomas Dekker

NIGHT AND DAY, BOTH SWEET THINGS

A NIGHTMARE

WHEN you're lying awake with a dismal headache, and
repose is taboo'd by anxiety,
I conceive you may use any language you choose to indulge
in without impropriety;
For your brain is on fire—the bedclothes conspire of usual
slumber to plunder you:
First your counterpane goes and uncovers your toes and
your sheet slips demurely from under you;
Then the blanketing tickles—you feel like mixed pickles,
so terribly sharp is the pricking,
And you're hot and you're cross, and you tumble and toss
till there's nothing 'twixt you and the ticking.
Then the bed-clothes all creep to the ground in a heap,
and you pick 'em all up in a tangle;
Next your pillow resigns and politely declines to remain
at its usual angle!
Well, you get some repose in the form of a doze, with hot
eyeballs and head ever aching,
But your slumbering teems with such horrible dreams that
you'd very much better be waking;
For you dream you are crossing the Channel, and tossing
about in a steamer from Harwich,
Which is something between a large bathing machine and
a very small second-class carriage:
And you're giving a treat (penny ice and cold meat) to a
party of friends and relations—
They're a ravenous hoard—and they all come on board at
Sloane Square and South Kensington Stations.
And bound on that journey you find your attorney (who
started that morning from Devon);
He's a bit undersized, and you don't feel surprised when
he tells you he's only eleven.
Well, you're driving like mad with this singular lad (by-
the-bye the ship's now a four-wheeler),
And you're playing round games, and he calls you bad
names when you tell him that 'ties pay the dealer;'
But this you can't stand, so you throw up your hand, and
you find you're as cold as an icicle,
In your shirt and your socks (the black silk with gold
clocks), crossing Salisbury Plain on a bicycle:

And he and the crew are on bicycles too—which they've
    somehow or other invested in—
And he's telling the tars all the particulárs of a company
    he's interésted in—
It's a scheme of devices, to get at low prices, all goods
    from cough mixture to cables,
(Which tickled the sailors) by treating retailers, as though
    they were all vegetábles—
You get a good tradesman to plant a small tradesman
    (first take off his boots with a boot-tree),
And his legs will take root, and his fingers will shoot, and
    they'll blossom and bud like a fruit-tree—
From the greengrocer tree you get grapes and green pea,
    cauliflower, pineapple and cranberries,
While the pastry-cook plant cherry brandy will grant,
    apple puffs, and three-corners, and banberries—
The shares are a penny, and ever so many are taken by
    ROTHSCHILD and BARING,
And just as a few are allotted to you, you awake with a
    shudder despairing—
You're a regular wreck, with a crick in your neck, and no wonder you
snore, for your head's on the floor, and you've needles and pins from
your soles to your shins, and your flesh is a-creep, for your left leg's
asleep, and you've cramp in your toes and a fly on your nose, and some
fluff in your lung, and a feverish tongue, and a thirst that's intense, and
a general sense that you haven't been sleeping in clover;

But the darkness has passed, and it's daylight at last, and the night has
been long—ditto, ditto my song—and thank goodness they're both of
them over!

Sir William Schwenck Gilbert

SLEEP

OH sleep! it is a gentle thing,
  Beloved from pole to pole!
To Mary Queen the praise be given!
She sent the gentle sleep from Heaven,
  That slid into my soul.

Samuel Taylor Coleridge, from The Rime of the Ancient Mariner

UP AND DOWN
THE WHOLE CREATION

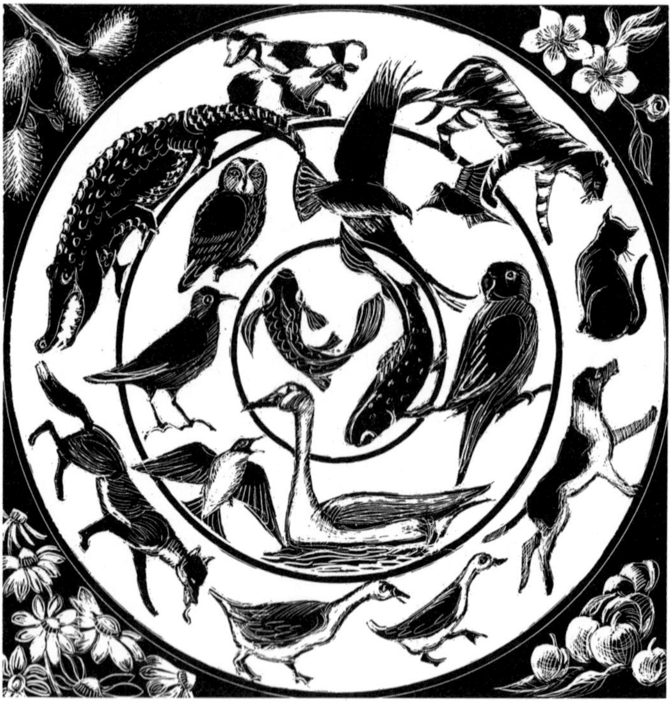

THE GARDEN

WHAT wondrous life is this I lead!
Ripe apples drop about my head;
The luscious clusters of the vine
Upon my mouth do crush their wine;
The nectarine and curious peach
Into my hands themselves do reach;
Stumbling on melons, as I pass,
Ensnared with flowers, I fall on grass.

Meanwhile the mind, from pleasure less,
Withdraws into its happiness;
The mind, that ocean where each kind
Does straight its own resemblance find;
Yet it creates, transcending these,
Far other worlds and other seas,
Annihilating all that's made
To a green thought in a green shade.

Here at the fountain's sliding foot
Or at some fruit-tree's mossy root,
Casting the body's vest aside
My soul into the boughs does glide:
There, like a bird, it sits and sings,
Then whets and claps its silver wings,
And, till prepared for longer flight,
Waves in its plumes the various light...

Such was the happy Garden-state
While man walked there without a mate:
After a place so pure and sweet,
What other help could yet be meet!
But 'twas beyond a mortal's share
To wander solitary there:
Two paradises 'twere in one,
To live in Paradise alone....

Andrew Marvell, from Thoughts in a Garden

PIED BEAUTY

GLORY be to God for dappled things—
  For skies of couple-colour as a brinded cow;
    For rose-moles all in stipple upon trout that swim;
Fresh-firecoal chestnut-falls; finches' wings;
  Landscape plotted and pierced—fold, fallow, and plough;
    And áll trádes, their gear and tackle and trim.

All things counter, original, spare, and strange;
  Whatever is fickle, freckled (who knows how?)
    With swift, slow; sweet, sour; addazzle, dim;
He fathers-forth whose beauty is past change:
      Praise him.

Gerard Manley Hopkins

SWEET SUFFOLK OWL

SWEET Suffolk Owl, so trimly dight
  With feathers like a lady bright,
Thou sing'st alone, sitting by night
    Te whit, Te whoo! Te whit! Te whit!

Thy note, that forth so freely rolls
With shrill command the mouse controls;
And sings a dirge for dying souls,
    Te whit, Te whoo! Te whit! Te whit!

Thomas Vautour

TO DAFFODILS

FAIR daffodils, we weep to see
  You haste away so soon:
As yet the early-rising sun
  Has not attain'd his noon.
    Stay, stay,
    Until the hastening day
      Has run
    But to the Even-song;
And, having pray'd together, we
    Will go with you along.

We have short time to stay, as you,
　　We have as short a Spring:
As quick a growth to meet Decay
　　As you, or anything.
　　　　We die,
As your hours do; and dry
　　　　Away
Like to the Summer's rain;
Or as the pearls of Morning's dew,
　　Ne'er to be found again.

Robert Herrick

THE NIGHTINGALE AND THE GLOW-WORM

A NIGHTINGALE that all day long
Had cheered the village with his song,
Nor yet at eve his note suspended,
Nor yet when eventide was ended,
Began to feel, as well he might,
The keen demands of appetite;
When looking eagerly around,
He spied far off, upon the ground,
A something shining in the dark,
And knew the Glowworm by his spark;
So, stooping down from hawthorn top,
He thought to put him in his crop.
The worm, aware of his intent,
Harrangued him thus, right eloquent:
'Did you admire my lamp,' quoth he,
'As much as I your minstrelsy,
You would abhor to do me wrong,
As much as I to spoil your song:
For 'twas the self-same Power Divine
Taught you to sing, and me to shine;
That you with music, I with light,
Might beautify and cheer the night.'
The songster heard this short oration,
And warbling out his approbation,
Released him, as my story tells,
And found a supper somewhere else.

William Cowper

THE PARROT

A TRUE STORY

A PARROT, from the Spanish main,
　Full young and early caged came o'er,
With bright wings, to the bleak domain
　　Of Mulla's shore.

To spicy groves where he had won
　His plumage of resplendent hue,
His native fruits, and skies, and sun,
　　He bade adieu.

For these he changed the smoke of turf,
　A heathery land and misty sky,
And turned on rocks and raging surf
　　His golden eye.

But petted in our climate cold,
　He lived and chattered many a day:
Until with age, from green and gold
　　His wings grew grey.

At last when blind, and seeming dumb,
　He scolded, laugh'd, and spoke no more,
A Spanish stranger chanced to come
　　To Mulla's shore;

He hail'd the bird in Spanish speech,
　The bird in Spanish speech replied;
Flapp'd round the cage with joyous screech,
　　Dropt down, and died.

Thomas Campbell

THE FOX

THE Fox went out one wintry night
　And prayed for the moon to give him light,
For he'd many a mile to go that night
　　Before he reached his Den O!
　　　　Den O! Den O!
For he'd many a mile to go that night
　　Before he reached his Den O!

UP AND DOWN THE WHOLE CREATION

And when he came to the old park gate,
    Where he'd often been both early and late,
It made his poor bones to shiver and shake,
    When he heard the full cry of the Hounds O!
          Hounds O! Hounds O!
It made his poor bones to shiver and shake
    When he heard the full cry of the Hounds O!

At last he came to a farmer's yard,
    Where the ducks and the geese to him were barred,
'Now the best of you shall grease my beard
    Before I leave the Farm O!
          Farm O! Farm O!
Now the best of you shall grease my beard
    Before I leave the Farm O!'

He grabbed the grey goose by the neck,
    And laid the duck across his back,
And he heeded not their quack-quack-quack,
    With their legs all dangling Down O!
          Down O! Down O !
And heeded not their quack-quack-quack
    With their legs all dangling Down O!

Old Mother Slipper-Slopper jumped out of bed,
    Down went the window and out popped her head,
Yelling, 'John, John, John, the grey goose is gone,
    And the Fox has gone over the Moor O!
          Moor O! Moor O!'
Yelling, 'John, John, John, the grey goose is gone,
    And the Fox has gone over the Moor O!'

Now John rushed up to the top of the hill,
    And blowed his horn both loud and shrill,
'Blow on,' said the Fox, 'Your pretty music still,
    Whilst I trot back to my Home O!
          Home O! Home O!'
'Blow on,' says the Fox, 'your pretty music still
    Whilst I trot back to my Home O!'

At last he reached his cosy little den,
    Where sat his young ones, eight, nine ten,
Quoth they, 'O Daddy, you must go there again,

>   For sure 'tis a lucky Town O!
> > Town O! Town O!'
> Quoth they, 'O Daddy, you must go there again,
> > For sure 'tis a lucky Town O!'

> Then the Fox and his wife without any strife,
> > They carved up the goose without fork or knife,
> And said, ' 'Twas the best they'd ever tasted in their life,'
> > And the little ones nibbled the bones O!
> > > Bones O! Bones O!
> And said: ' 'Twas the best they'd ever tasted in their life,'
> > And the little ones nibbled the bones O!

Traditional

JOHN PEEL

D'YE ken John Peel with his coat so gay?
D'ye ken John Peel at the break of the day?
D'ye ken John Peel when he's far, far away,
With his hounds and his horn in the morning?

> *'Twas the sound of his horn called me from my bed,*
> *And the cry of his hounds has me oft-times led,*
> *For Peel's View-hollo would waken the dead,*
> *Or a fox from his lair in the morning.*

D'ye ken that bitch whose tongue is death?
D'ye ken her sons of peerless faith?
D'ye ken that a fox with his last breath
Curs'd them all as he died in the morning? *(chorus)*

Yes, I ken John Peel and Ruby too,
Ranter and Royal and Bellman as true;
From the drag to the chase, from the chase to a view,
From a view to the death in the morning. *(chorus)*

And I've followed John Peel both often and far
O'er the rasper-fence and the gate and the bar,
From Low Denton Holme up to Scratchmere Scar,
When we vied for the brush in the morning.*(chorus)*

Then here's to John Peel with my heart and soul,
Come fill—fill to him another strong bowl:

And we'll follow John Peel through fair and through foul,
While we're waked by his horn in the morning. *(chorus)*

John Woodcock Graves

THE LITTLE CROCODILE

HOW doth the little crocodile
 Improve his shining tail,
And pour the waters of the Nile
 On every golden scale!

How cheerfully he seems to grin,
 How neatly spreads his claws,
And welcomes little fishes in,
 With gently smiling jaws!

Lewis Carroll, from Alice in Wonderland

THE EAGLE

HE clasps the crag with crooked hands;
 Close to the sun in lonely lands,
Ring'd with the azure world, he stands.

The wrinkled sea beneath him crawls;
He watches from his mountain walls,
And like a thunderbolt he falls.

Alfred, Lord Tennyson

THE SILVER SWAN

THE silver swan, who living had no note,
 When death approached unlocked her silent throat.
Leaning her breast against the reedy shore
Thus sung her first and last and sung no more:
Farewell all joys, O Death, come close mine eyes,
More geese than swans now live, more fools than wise.

Anon—set to music by Orlando Gibbons

CAT JEOFFRY

FOR I will consider my Cat Jeoffry.
For he is the servant of the Living God, duly and daily serving Him.
For at the first glance of the glory of God in the East he worships in his way.
For this is done by wreathing his body seven times round with elegant quickness.
For then he leaps up to catch the musk, which is the blessing of God upon his prayer.
For he rolls upon prank to work it in.
For having done duty & received blessing he begins to consider himself.
For this he performs in ten degrees.
For first he looks at his fore-paws to see if they are clean.
For secondly he kicks up behind to clear away there.
For thirdly he works it upon stretch with the fore-paws extended.
For fourthly he sharpens his claws by wood.
For fifthly he washes himself.
For sixthly he rolls upon wash.
For seventhly he fleas himself, that he may not be interrupted upon the beat.
For eighthly he rubs himself against a post.
For ninthly he looks up for his instructions.
For tenthly he goes in quest of food.
For having consider'd God and himself he will consider his neighbour.
For if he meets another cat he will kiss her in kindness.
For when he takes his prey he plays with it to give it a chance.
For one mouse in seven escapes by his dallying.
For when his day's work is done his business more properly begins.
For he keeps the Lord's watch in the night against the adversary.
For he counteracts the powers of darkness by his electrical skin And glaring eyes.
For he counteracts the Devil, who is death, by brisking about the life.
For in his morning orisons he loves the sun & the sun loves him.
For he is of the tribe of Tiger.
For the Cherub cat is a term of the Angel Tiger.
For he has the subtlety & hissing of a serpent which in goodness he suppresses,
For he will not do destruction, if he is well-fed, neither will he spit

without provocation,
For he purrs in thankfulness, when God tells him he is a good Cat.
For he is an instrument for the children to learn benevolence upon.
For every house is incomplete without him & a blessing is lacking in the spirit.

Christopher Smart.

THE FISH

IN a cool curving world he lies
And ripples with dark ecstasies.
The kind luxurious lapse and steal
Shapes all his universe to feel
And know and be; the clinging stream
Closes his memory, glooms his dream,
Who lips the roots o' the shore, and glides
Superb on unreturning tides.
Those silent waters weave for him
A fluctuant mutable world and dim,
Where wavering masses bulge and gape
Mysterious, and shape to shape
Dies momently through whorl and hollow,
Solid and line and form to dream
Fantastic down the eternal stream;
An obscure world, a shifting world,
Bulbous, or pulled to thin, or curled,
Or serpentine, or driving arrows,
Or serene slidings, or March narrows.
There slipping wave and shore are one,
And weed and mud. No ray of sun,
But glow to glow fades down the deep
(As dream to unknown dream in sleep);
Shaken translucency illumes
The hyaline of drifting glooms;
The strange soft-handed depth subdues
Drowned colour there, but black to hues
As death to living, decomposes—
Red darkness of the heart of roses,
Blue brilliant from dead starless skies,
And gold that lies behind the eyes,
The unknown unnameable sightless white

That is the essential flame of night,
Lustreless purple, hooded green,
The myriad hues that lie between
Darkness and darkness!...
                    And all's one,
Gentle, embracing, quiet, dun,
The world he rests in, world he knows,
Perpetual curving. Only—grows
An eddy in that ordered falling,
A knowledge from the gloom, a calling
Weed in the wave, gleam in the mud—
The dark fire leaps along his blood;
Dateless and deathless, blind and still,
The intricate impulse works its will;
His woven world drops back and he,
Sans providence, sans memory,
Unconscious and directly driven,
Fades to some dank sufficient heaven.

O world of lips, O world of laughter,
Where hope is fleet and thought flies after,
Of lights in the clear night, of cries
That drift along the wave and rise
Thin to the glittering stars above,
You know the hands, the eyes of love!
The strife of limbs, the sightless clinging,
The infinite distance, and the singing
Blown by the wind, a flame of sound,
The gleam, the flowers, and vast around
The horizon, and the heights above—
You know the sigh, the song of love!...
Space is no more, under the mud;
His bliss is older than the sun.
Silent and straight, the waters run,
The lights, the cries, the willows dim,
And the dark tide are one with him.

Rupert Brooke

ON A FAVOURITE CAT DROWNED

'TWAS on a lofty vase's side
Where China's gayest art had dyed
    The azure flowers that blow;
Demurest of the tabby kind,
The pensive Selima, reclined,
    Gazed on the lake below.

Her conscious tail her joy declared;
The fair round face, the snowy beard,
    The velvet of her paws,
Her coat, that with the tortoise vies,
Her ears of jet, and emerald eyes,
    She saw, and purr'd applause.

Still had she gazed, but 'midst the tide
Two angel forms were seen to glide,
    The Genii of the stream:
Their scaly armour's Tyrian hue,
Thro' richest purple, to the view
    Betray'd a golden gleam.

The hapless Nymph with wonder saw:
A whisker first, and then a claw,
    With many an ardent wish,
She stretch'd in vain to reach the prize.
What female heart can gold despise?
    What Cat's averse to fish?

Presumptious maid! with looks intent
Again she stretch'd, again she bent,
    Nor knew the gulf between.
(Malignant fate sat by, and smiled.)
The slipp'ry verge her feet beguiled,
    She tumbled headlong in.

Eight times emerging from the flood
She mew'd to every watery god,
    Some speedy aid to send.
No Dolphin came, no Nereid stirr'd,
Nor cruel Tom nor Susan heard—
    A favourite has no friend!

From hence, ye Beauties undeceived,
Know, one false step is ne'er retrieved,
   And be with caution bold.
Not all that tempts your wand'ring eyes
And heedless hearts, is lawful prize;
   Not all that glisters, gold.

Thomas Gray

AN ELEGY ON THE DEATH OF A MAD DOG

GOOD people all, of every sort,
   Give ear unto my song;
And if you find it wondrous short,—
   It cannot hold you long.

In Islington there was a man,
   Of whom the world might say,
That still a godly race he ran,—
   Whene'er he went to pray.

A kind and gentle heart he had,
   To comfort friends and foes;
The naked every day he clad,—
   When he put on his clothes.

And in that town a dog was found,
   As many dogs there be,
Both mongrel, puppy, whelp, and hound,
   And curs of low degree.

This dog and man at first were friends;
   But when a pique began,
The dog, to gain his private ends,
   Went mad, and bit the man.

Around from all the neighbouring streets
   The wondering neighbours ran,
And swore the dog had lost its wits,
   To bite so good a man.

The wound it seem'd both sore and sad
   To every Christian eye;

And while they swore the dog was mad,
   They swore the man would die.

But soon a wonder came to light,
   That show'd the rogues they lied;
The man recovered of the bite,
   The dog it was that died.

Oliver Goldsmith

THE LARK ASCENDING

HE rises and begins to round,
He drops the silver chain of sound,
Of many links without a break,
In chirrup, whistle, slur and shake,
All intervolved and spreading wide,
Like water-dimples down a tide
Where ripple ripple overcurls
And eddy into eddy whirls;
A press of hurried notes that run
So fleet they scarce are more than one,
Yet changeingly the trills repeat
And linger ringing while they fleet,
Sweet to the quick o' the ear, and dear
To her beyond the handmaid ear,
Who sits beside our inner springs,
Too often dry for this he brings,
Which seems the very jet of earth
At sight of sun, her music's mirth,
As up he wings the spiral stair,
A song of light, and pierces air
With fountain ardour, fountain play,
To reach the shining tops of day,
And drink in everything discerned
An ecstasy to music turned,
Impelled by what his happy bill
Disperses; drinking, showering still,
Unthinking save that he may give
His voice the outlet, there to live
Renewed in endless notes of glee,
So thirsty of his voice is he,
For all to hear and all to know

That he is joy, awake, aglow,
The tumult of the heart to hear
Through pureness filtered crystal-clear,
And know the pleasure sprinkled bright
By simple singing of delight,
Shrill, irreflective, unrestrained,
Rapt, ringing, on the jet sustained
Without a break, without a fall,
Sweet-silvery, sheer lyrical,
Perennial, quavering up the chord
Like myriad dews of sunny sward
That trembling into fulness shine,
And sparkle dropping argentine;
Such wooing as the ear receives
From zephyr caught in choric leaves
Of aspens when their chattering net
Is flushed to white with shivers wet;
And such the water-spirit's chime
On mountain heights in morning's prime,
Too freshly sweet to seem excess,
Too animate to need a stress;
But wider over many heads
The starry voice ascending spreads,
Awakening, as it waxes thin,
The best in us to him akin;
And every face to watch him raised,
Puts on the light of children praised,
So rich our human pleasure ripes
When sweetness on sincereness pipes,
Though nought be promised from the seas,
But only a soft-ruffling breeze
Sweep glittering on a still content,
Serenity in ravishment…

George Meredith, extract from The Lark Ascending

SONG

I HAD a dove, and the sweet dove died;
And I have thought it died of grieving:
O, what could it grieve for? Its feet were tied
    With a silken thread of my own hand's weaving;
Sweet little red feet! why should you die—
Why should you leave me, sweet bird! why?
You lived alone in the forest-tree,
Why, pretty thing! would you not live with me?
I kiss'd you oft and gave you white peas;
Why not live sweetly, as in the green trees?

John Keats

THE TIGER

TIGER! Tiger! burning bright
  In the forests of the night,
What immortal hand or eye
Could frame thy fearful symmetry?

In what distant deeps or skies
Burnt the fire of thine eyes?
On what wings dare he aspire?
What the hand dare seize the fire?

And what shoulder, and what art
Could twist the sinews of thy heart?
And when thy heart began to beat,
What dread hand? and what dread feet?

What the hammer? what the chain?
In what furnace was thy brain?
What the anvil? what dread grasp
Dare its deadly terrors clasp?

When the stars threw down their spears,
And water'd heaven with their tears,
Did He smile His work to see?
Did He who made the Lamb make thee?

William Blake

THE JACKDAW OF RHEIMS

THE Jackdaw sat on the Cardinal's chair!
Bishop and abbot and prior were there;
 Many a monk, and many a friar,
 Many a knight and many a squire,
With a great many more of lesser degree,—
In sooth a goodly company;
And they served the Lord Primate on bended knee.
 Never, I ween, Was a prouder seen,
Read of in books, or dreamt of in dreams,
Than the Cardinal Lord Archbishop of Rheims.

 In and out Through the motley rout,
The little Jackdaw kept hopping about;
 Here and there Like a dog in a fair,
 Over comfits and cakes, And dishes and plates,
Cowl and cope, and rochet, and pall,
Mitre and crozier! he hopp'd upon all!
 With a saucy air, He perch'd on the chair
Where, in state, the great Lord Cardinal sat
In the great Lord Cardinal's great red hat;
 And he peer'd in the face Of his Lordship's Grace,
With a satisfied look, as if he would say,
'We two are the greatest folks here today!'
 And the priests, with awe, As such freaks they saw,
Said, 'The Devil must be in that little Jackdaw.'

The feast was over, the board was clear'd,
The flawns and the custards had all disappear'd,
And six little Singing-boys,—dear little souls!
In nice clean faces, and nice white stoles,
 Came, in order due, Two by two
Marching the great refectory through!
A nice little boy held a golden ewer,
Emboss'd and fill'd with water, as pure
As any that flows between Rheims and Namur,
Which a nice little boy stood ready to catch
In a fine golden hand-basin made to match.
Two nice little boys, rather more grown,
Carried lavender-water, and eau de Cologne,
And a nice little boy had a nice cake of soap,

UP AND DOWN THE WHOLE CREATION

Worthy of washing the hands of the Pope.
    One little boy more   A napkin bore,
Of the best white diaper, fringed with pink,
And a Cardinal's hat mark'd in 'permanent ink.'

The great Lord Cardinal turns at the sight
Of these nice little boys dress'd all in white:
    From his fingers he draws   His costly turquoise;
And, not thinking at all about little Jackdaws,
    Deposits it straight   By the side of his plate,
While the nice little boys on his Eminence wait;
Till, when nobody's dreaming of any such thing,
That little Jackdaw hops off with the ring!

    There's a cry and a shout,   And a deuce of a rout,
And nobody seems to know what they're about,
But the monks have their pockets all turn'd inside out;
    The friars are kneeling,   And hunting, and feeling
The carpet, the floor, and the walls, and the ceiling.
    The Cardinal drew   Off each plum-colour'd shoe,
And left his red stockings exposed to the view;
    He peeps and he feels   In the toes and the heels;
They turn up the dishes,—they turn up the plates,—
They take up the poker and poke out the grates,
    —They turn up the rugs,   They examine the mugs:—
    But no!—no such thing;   —They can't find THE RING!
And the Abbott declared that, 'When nobody twigg'd it,
Some rascal or other had popp'd in and prigg'd it'

The Cardinal rose with a dignified look,
He call'd for his candle, his bell, and his book!
    In holy anger and pious grief,
    He solemnly cursed that rascally thief!
    He cursed him at board, he cursed him in bed;
    From the sole of his foot to the crown of his head;
    He cursed him in sleeping, that every night
    He should dream of the devil, and wake in a fright;
    He cursed him in eating, he cursed him in drinking,
    He cursed him in coughing, in sneezing, in winking;
    He cursed him in sitting, in standing, in lying;
    He cursed him in walking, in riding, in flying,
    He cursed him in living, he cursed him in dying!—

Never was heard such a terrible curse!
    But what gave rise   To no little surprise,
Nobody seem'd one penny the worse!

    The day was gone,   The night came on,
The Monks and the Friars they search'd till dawn;
    When the sacristan saw,   On crumpled claw,
Come limping a poor little lame Jackdaw!
    No longer gay,   As on yesterday;
His feathers all seem'd to be turn'd the wrong way;—
His pinions droop'd—he could hardly stand,—
His head was as bald as the palm of your hand;
    His eyes so dim,   So wasted each limb,
That, heedless of grammar, they all cried, 'THAT'S HIM!—
That's the scamp that has done this scandalous thing!
That's the thief who has got my Lord Cardinal's Ring!'
    The poor little Jackdaw,   When the monks he saw,
Feebly gave vent to the ghost of a caw;
And turn'd his bald head, as much as to say;
'Pray be so good as to walk this way!'
    Slower and slower   He limped on before,
    Where the first thing they saw,   'Midst the sticks and the straw,
Was the RING in the nest of that little Jackdaw!

Then the great Lord Cardinal call'd for his book,
And off that terrible curse he took;
    The mute expression   Served in lieu of confession,
And, being thus coupled with full restitution,
The Jackdaw got plenary absolution!
    —When those words were heard,   That poor little bird
Was so changed in a moment, 'twas really absurd,
    He grew sleek, and fat,   In addition to that,
A fresh crop of feathers came thick as a mat!
    His tail waggled more   Even than before;
But no longer it waggled with an impudent air,
No longer he perch'd on the Cardinal's chair.
    He hopp'd now about   With a gait devout;
At Matins, at Vespers, he never was out;
And, so far from any more pilfering deeds,
He always seem'd telling the Confessor's beads.
If any one lied,—or if any one swore,—
Or slumber'd in prayer-time and happen'd to snore,

That good Jackdaw,   Would give a great 'Caw!'
As much as to say, 'Don't do so any more!'
While many remark'd, as his manners they saw,
That they 'never had known such a pious Jackdaw!'
    He had long lived the pride   Of that country side,
And at last in the odour of sanctity died;
    When, as words were too faint,   His merits to paint,
The Conclave determined to make him a Saint;
And on newly-made Saints and Popes, as you know,
It's the custom, at Rome, new names to bestow,
So they canonized him by the name of Jim Crow.

Richard Harris Barham

PSALM NINETEEN

THE heavens declare the glory of God;
    And the firmament sheweth his handiwork.
Day unto day uttereth speech,
    And night unto night sheweth knowledge.
There is no speech nor language,
    Where their voice is not heard.
Their line is gone out through all the earth,
    And their words to the end of the world.

    In them hath he set a tabernacle for the sun,
Which is as a bridegroom coming out of his chamber,
    And rejoiceth as a strong man to run a race.
His going forth is from the end of the heaven,
    And his circuit unto the ends of it:
And there is nothing hid from the heat thereof.

The law of the Lord is perfect,
    Converting the soul:
The testimony of the Lord is sure,
    Making wise the simple.
The statutes of the Lord are right,
    Rejoicing the heart:
The commandment of the Lord is pure,
    Enlightening the eyes.
The fear of the Lord is clean,
    Enduring for ever:
The judgements of the Lord are true

    And righteous altogether.
More to be desired are they than gold,
    Yea, than much fine gold:
Sweeter also than honey
    And the honeycomb.
Moreover by them is thy servant warned:
    And in keeping of them there is great reward.

Who can understand his errors?
    Cleanse thou me from secret faults.
Keep back thy servant from presumptuous sins;
    Let them not have dominion over me:
Then shall I be upright, and I shall be innocent
    From the great transgression.

Let the words of my mouth,
    And the meditation of my heart,
Be acceptable in thy sight,
    O Lord, my strength, and my redeemer.

The Holy Bible

GOD'S GRANDEUR

THE world is charged with the grandeur of God.
  It will flame out, like shining from shook foil;
  It gathers to a greatness, like the ooze of oil
Crushed. Why do men then now not reck his rod?
Generations have trod, have trod, have trod;
    And all is seared with trade; bleared, smeared with toil;
    And wears man's smudge and shares man's smell: the soil
Is bare now, nor can foot feel, being shod.

And for all this, nature is never spent;
    There lives the dearest freshness deep down things;
And though the last lights off the black West went
    Oh, morning, at the brown brink eastward, springs—
Because the Holy Ghost over the bent
    World broods with warm breast and with ah! bright wings.

Gerard Manley Hopkins

BLOW, BUGLE, BLOW

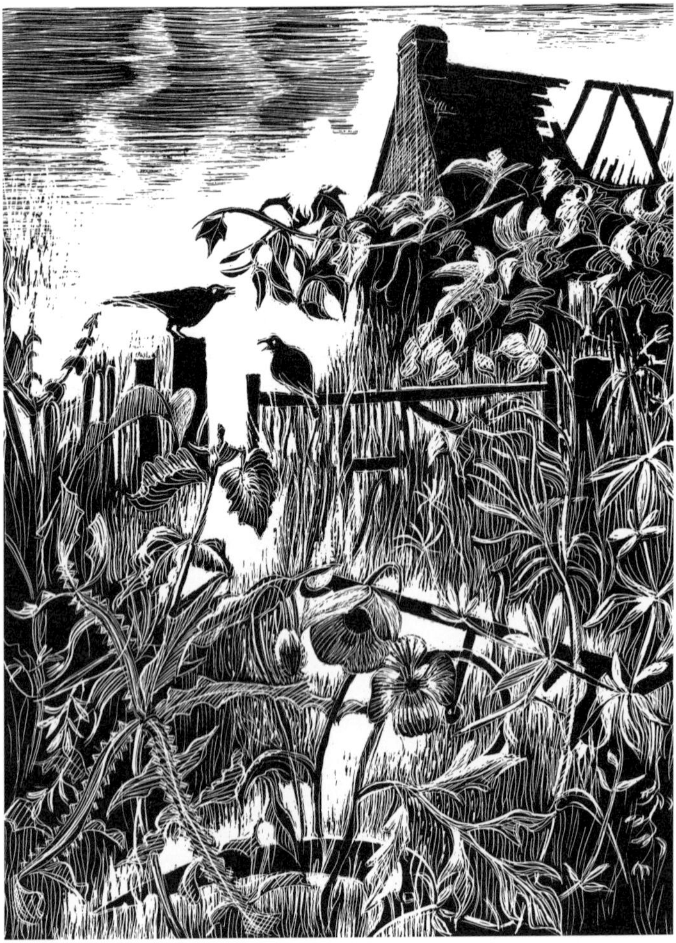

THE CHARGE OF THE LIGHT BRIGADE

Half a league, half a league,
Half a league onward,
All in the valley of Death
   Rode the six hundred.
'Forward, the Light Brigade!
Charge for the guns!' he said:
Into the valley of Death
   Rode the six handred.

'Forward, the Light Brigade!'
Was there a man dismay'd?
Not tho' the soldier knew
   Someone had blunder'd:
Theirs not to make reply,
Theirs not to reason why,
Theirs but to do and die:
Into the valley of Death
   Road the six hundred.

Cannon to right of them,
Cannon to left of them,
Cannon in front of them
   Volley'd and thunder'd;
Storm'd at with shot and shell,
Boldly they rode and well,
Into the jaws of Death,
Into the mouth of Hell
   Rode the six hundred.

Flash'd all their sabres bare,
Flash'd as they turn'd in air
Sabring the gunners there,
Charging an army, while
   All the world wonder'd:
Plunged in the battery-smoke,
Right thro' the line they broke;
Cossack and Russian
Reel'd from the sabre-stroke
   Shatter'd and sunder'd.
Then they rode back, but not
   Not the six hundred.

Cannon to right of them,
Cannon to left of them,
Cannon behind them
   Volley'd and thunder'd;
Storm'd at with shot and shell,
While horse and hero fell,
They that had fought so well
Came thro' the jaws of Death,
Back from the mouth of Hell,
All that was left of them,
   Left of six hundred.

When can their glory fade?
O the wild charge they made!
   All the world wonder'd.
Honour the charge they made!
Honour the Light Brigade,
   Noble six hundred!

Alfred, Lord Tennyson

THE AGINCOURT SONG

OUR King went forth to Normandy,
With grace and might of chivalry:
There God for him wrought marv'lously,
Wherefore England may call and cry:
   Deo gratias, Deo gratias,
   Anglia redde pro victoria.

He set a siegè the sooth for to say,
To Harfleur town with royal array:
That town he won, and made a fray
That France shall rue till Doomesday. *(chorus)*

Then went our King with all his host
Through France for all the Frenchè boast:
He spared no dread of least or most,
Till he came to Agincourt coast. *(chorus)*

Then, for a sooth, that knight comely,
In Agincourt field he fought manly:
Through grace of God most mighty,
He had both the field and the victory. *(chorus)*

There dukes and earls, lord and baron,
Were taken and slain, and that well done:
And some were led into London,
With joy and mirth and great renown. (*chorus*)

Now gracious God, He save our King,
His people and all his well willing:
Give him good life and good ending,
That we with mirth may safely sing: (*chorus*)

Anon

KING HENRY, TO HIS TROOPS BEFORE HARFLEUR

ONCE more unto the breach, dear friends, once more;
Or close the wall up with our English dead.
In peace there's nothing so becomes a man
As modest stillness and humility;
But when the blast of war blows in our ears,
Then imitate the action of the tiger:
Stiffen the sinews, summon up the blood,
Disguise fair nature with hard-favour'd rage;
Then lend the eye a terrible aspect;
Let it pry through the portage of the head
Like the brass cannon; let the brow o'erwhelm it
As fearfully as doth a galled rock
O'erhang and jutty his confounded base,
Swill'd with the wild and wasteful ocean.
Now set the teeth and stretch the nostril wide;
Hold hard the breath, and bend up every spirit
To his full height. On, on, you noblest English,
Whose blood is fet from fathers of war-proof—
Fathers that like so many Alexanders
Have in these parts from morn till even fought,
And sheath'd their swords for lack of argument.
Dishonour not your mothers; now attest
That those whom you call'd fathers did beget you.
Be copy now to men of grosser blood,
And teach them how to war. And you, good yeomen,
Whose limbs were made in England, show us here
The mettle of your pasture; let us swear
That you are worth your breeding—which I doubt not;
For there is none of you so mean and base

That hath not noble lustre in your eyes.
I see you stand like greyhounds in the slips,
Straining upon the start. The game's afoot:
Follow your spirit; and upon this charge
Cry 'God for Harry, England, and Saint George!'

William Shakespeare, from King Henry the Fifth

HORATIUS

LARS PORSENA of Clusium
By the Nine Gods he swore
That the wronged house of Tarquin
Should suffer wrong no more.
By the Nine Gods he swore it,
And named a trysting day,
And bade his messengers ride forth,
East and west and south and north,
To summon his array.

And now hath every city
Sent up her tale of men;
The foot are fourscore thousand,
The horse are thousands ten.
Before the gate of Sutrium
Is met the great array.
A proud man was Lars Porsena
Upon the trysting day.

But by the yellow Tiber
Was tumult and affright;
From all the spacious champaign
To Rome men took their flight.
A mile around the city
The throng stopped up the ways;
A fearful sight it was to see
Through two long nights and days.

To eastward and to westward
Have spread the Tuscan bands;
Nor house, nor fence, nor dovecote
In Crustumerium stands.
Verbenna down to Ostia

Hath wasted all the plain;
Astur hath stormed Janiculum,
And the stout guards are slain.

They held a council standing
Before the River-Gate;
Short time was there, ye well may guess,
For musing and debate.
Out spake the Consul roundly:
'The bridge must straight go down;
For, since Janiculum is lost,
Nought else can save the town.'

But the Consul's brow was sad,
And the Consul's speech was low,
And darkly looked he at the wall,
And darkly at the foe.
'Their van will be upon us
Before the bridge goes down;
And if they once may win the bridge,
What hope to save the town?'

Then out spake brave Horatius,
The Captain of the gate:
'To every man upon this earth
Death cometh soon or late;
And how can man die better
Than facing fearful odds,
For the ashes of his fathers
And the temples of his gods?

Hew down the bridge, Sir Consul,
With all the speed ye may;
I, with two more to help me,
Will hold the foe in play.
In yon strait path a thousand
May well be stopped by three.
Now who will stand on either hand
And keep the bridge with me?'

Then out spake Spurius Lartius;
A Ramnian proud was he:
'Lo, I will stand at thy right hand,

And keep the bridge with thee.'
And out spake strong Herminius;
Of Titian blood was he:
'I will abide on thy left side,
And keep the bridge with thee.'

Now while the Three were tightening
Their harness on their backs,
The Consul was the foremost man
To take in hand an axe:
And Fathers mixed with Commons
Seized hatchet, bar, and crow,
And smote upon the planks above,
And loosed the props below.

The Three stood calm and silent
And looked upon the foes,
And a great shout of laughter
From all the vanguard rose:
And forth three chiefs came spurring
Before that deep array;
To earth they sprang, their swords they drew,
And lifted high their shields, and flew
To win the narrow way;

Stout Lartius hurled down Aunus
Into the stream beneath:
Herminius struck at Seius,
And clove him to the teeth:
At Picus brave Horatius
Darted one fiery thrust;
And the proud Umbrian's gilded arms
Clashed in the bloody dust.

But now no sound of laughter
Was heard among the foes.
A wild and wrathful clamour
From all the vanguard rose.
Six spears' lengths from the entrance
Halted the deep array,
And for a space no man came forth
To win the narrow way.

Was none who would be foremost
To lead such dire attack;
But those behind cried 'Foreward!'
And those before cried 'Back!'
And backward now and forward
Wavers the deep array;
And on the tossing sea of steel,
To and fro the standards reel;
And the victorious trumpet-peal
Dies fitfully away.

But meanwhile axe and lever
Have manfully been plied;
And now the bridge hangs tottering
Above the boiling tide.
'Come back, come back, Horatius!'
Loud cried the Fathers all.
'Back, Laertius! back, Herminius!
Back ere the ruin fall!'

Back darted Spurius Lartius;
Herminius darted back:
And, as they passed, beneath their feet
They felt the timbers crack.
But when they turned their faces,
And on the farther shore
Saw brave Horatius stand alone,
They would have crossed once more.

But with a crash of thunder
Fell every loosened beam,
And, like a dam, the mighty wreck
Lay right athwart the stream:
And a long shout of triumph
Rose from the walls of Rome;
As to the highest turret-tops
Was splashed the yellow foam.

Alone stood brave Horatius,
But constant still in mind;
Thrice thirty thousand foes before,
And the broad flood behind.
'Down with him!' cried false Sextus,

With a smile on his pale face.
'Now yield thee,' cried Lars Porsena,
'Now yield thee to our grace.'

Round turned he, as not deigning
Those craven ranks to see;
Nought spake he to Lars Porsena,
To Sextus nought spake he;
But he saw on Palatinus
The white porch of his home;
And he spake to the noble river
That rolls by the towers of Rome.

'O Tiber! father Tiber!
To whom the Romans pray,
A Roman's life, a Roman's arms,
Take thou in charge this day!'
So he spake, and speaking sheathed
The good sword by his side,
And with his harness on his back,
Plunged headlong in the tide.

No sound of joy or sorrow
Was heard from either bank;
But friends and foes in dumb surprise
With parted lips and straining eyes,
Stood gazing where he sank;
And when above the surges
They saw his crest appear,
All Rome sent forth a rapturous cry,
And even the ranks of Tuscany
Could scarce forbear to cheer.

But fiercely ran the current,
Swollen high by months of rain:
And fast his blood was flowing;
And he was sore in pain,
And heavy with his armour,
And spent with changing blows:
And oft they thought him sinking,
But still again he rose.

And now he feels the bottom;
Now on dry earth he stands;
Now round him throng the Fathers
To press his gory hands;
And now with shouts and clapping,
And noise of weeping loud,
He enters through the River-Gate,
Borne by the joyous crowd.

And in the nights of winter,
When the cold north winds blow,
And the howling of the wolves
Is heard amidst the snow;
When round the lonely cottage
Roars loud the tempest din,
And the good logs of Algidus
Roar louder yet within;

When the goodman mends his armour
And trims his helmet's plume;
When the goodwife's shuttle merrily
Goes flashing through the loom;
With weeping and with laughter
Still is the story told,
How well Horatius kept the bridge
In the brave days of old.

Thomas Babington, Lord Macaulay, abridged from Lays of Ancient Rome

EGYPT'S MIGHT

EGYPT'S might is tumbled down
    Down a-down the deeps of thought;
Greece is fallen and Troy town,
Glorious Rome hath lost her crown,
    Venice's pride is nought.

But the dreams their children dreamed
    Fleeting, insubstantial, vain,
Shadowy as the shadows seemed,
Airy nothing, as they deemed,
    These remain.

Mary Elizabeth Coleridge

THE DESTRUCTION OF SENNACHERIB

THE Assyrian came down like the wolf on the fold,
And his cohorts were gleaming in purple and gold;
And the sheen of their spears was like stars on the sea,
When the blue wave rolls nightly on deep Galilee.

Like the leaves of the forest when Summer is green,
That host with their banners at sunset were seen:
Like leaves of the forest when Autumn hath blown,
That host on the morrow lay wither'd and strown.

For the Angel of Death spread his wings on the blast,
And breathed in the face of the foe as he pass'd;
And the eyes of the sleepers wax'd deadly and chill,
And their hearts but once heaved, and for ever grew still!

And there lay the steed with his nostril all wide,
But through them there roll'd not the breath of his pride;
And the foam of his gasping lay white on the turf,
And cold as the spray of the rock-beating surf.

And there lay the rider, distorted and pale,
With dew on his brow, and the rust on his mail:
And the tents were all silent, the banners alone,
The lances unlifted, the trumpet unblown.

And the widows of Ashur are loud in their wail,
And the idols are broke in the temple of Baal,
And the might of the Gentile, unsmote by the sword,
Hath melted like snow in the glance of the Lord!

George Gordon, Lord Byron

THE WAR-SONG OF DINAS VAWR

THE mountain sheep are sweeter,
But the valley sheep are fatter;
We therefore deemed it meeter
To carry off the latter.
We made an expedition;
We met a host, and quelled it;
We forced a strong position,
And killed the men who held it.

On Dyfed's richest valley,
Where herds of kine were browsing,
We made a mighty sally,
To furnish our carousing.
Fierce warriors rushed to meet us;
We met them, and o'erthrew them:
They struggled hard to beat us;
But we conquered them, and slew them.

As we drove our prize at leisure,
The king marched forth to catch us:
His rage surpassed all measure,
But his people could not match us.
He fled to his hall-pillars;
And, ere our force we led off,
Some sacked his house and cellars,
While others cut his head off.

We there, in strife bewild'ring,
Spilt blood enough to swim in:
We orphaned many children,
And widowed many women,
The eagles and the ravens
We glutted with our foemen;
The heroes and the cravens,
The spearmen and the bowmen.

We brought away from battle,
And much their land bemoaned them,
Two thousand head of cattle,
And the head of him who owned them.
Ednyfed, king of Dyfed,
His head was borne before us;
His wine and beasts supplied our feasts,
And his overthrow, our chorus.

Thomas Love Peacock

TO LUCASTA, ON GOING TO THE WARS

TELL me not, Sweet, I am unkind,
   That from the nunnery
Of thy chaste breast and quiet mind
   To war and arms I fly.

True, a new mistress now I chase,
   The first foe in the field;
And with a stronger faith embrace
   A sword, a horse, a shield.

Yet this inconstancy is such
   As thou too shall adore;
I could not love thee, Dear, so much,
   Loved I not Honour more.

Richard Lovelace

THE MINSTREL BOY

THE Minstrel Boy to the war is gone,
   In the ranks of death you'll find him;
His father's sword he has girded on,
   And his wild harp slung behind him;
'Land of song,' said the warrior bard,
   'Tho' all the world betray thee,
One sword at least thy rights shall guard,
   One faithful harp shall praise thee!'

The Minstrel fell! but the foeman's chain
   Could not bring that proud soul under;
The harp he lov'd ne'er spoke again,
   For he tore its cords asunder;
And he said, 'No chain shall sully thee,
   Thou soul of love and bravery!
Thy songs were made for the pure and free,
   They ne'er shall sound in slavery!'

Thomas Moore

MEN OF HARLECH

RHYFELGYRCH GWYR HARLECH

MEN of Harlech, march to glory,
Victory is hov'ring o'er ye,
Bright-eyed freedom stands before ye,
   Hear ye not her call?
At your sloth she seems to wonder,
Rend the sluggish bonds asunder,
Let the war-cry's deaf'ning thunder,
   Ev'ry foe appal.

Echoes loudly waking,
Hill and valley shaking;
Till the sound spreads wide around,
The Saxon's courage breaking;
Your foes on ev'ry side assailing,
Forward press with hearts unfailing,
Till invaders learn with quailing,
   Cambria ne'er can yield.

Thou who noble Cambria wrongest
Know that freedom's cause is strongest,
Freedom's courage lasts the longest,
   Ending but with death!
Freedom countless hosts can scatter,
Freedom stoutest mail can shatter,
Freedom thickest walls can batter,
   Fate is in her breath.

See they now are flying!
Dead are heap'd with dying!
Over might hath triumphed right,
Our land to foes denying:
Upon their soil we never sought them,
Love of conquest hither brought them,
But this lesson we have taught them,
   Cambria ne'er can yield.

   Weslsh Traditional, with English words by John Oxenford

THE HUNDRED PIPERS

Wi' a hundred pipers an' a', an' a',
Wi' a hundred pipers an' a', an' a',
We'll up an' gie 'em a blaw, a blaw.
Wi' a hundred pipers an' a', an' a'.

Oh it's ower the Border a-wa', a-wa',
It's ower the Border a-wa', a-wa',
We'll on an' we'll march to Carlisle, Ha',
Wi' its yetts, its castel, an 'a, an' a'. *(chorus)*

Oh! our sodger lads look'd braw, look'd braw,
Wi' their tartans, kilts, an' a', an' a',
Wi' their bonnets, an' feathers an' glitt'ring gear,
An' pibrochs sounding sweet an' clear.
Will they a' return—our Hieland men?
Second sighted Sandy look'd fu' wae,
And mothers grat when they march'd awa'. *(chorus)*

Oh wha is foremaist o' a', o' a'?
Oh wha does follow the blaw, the blaw?
Bonnie Charlie, the king o' us, hurra!
Wi' his hundred pipers an' a', an' a'!
His bonnet an' feather he's wavin' high!
His prancing steed maist seems to fly!
The nor' wind plays wi' his curly hair,
While the pipers blaw in an unco flare! *(chorus)*

The Esk was swollen, sae red, sae deep;
But shoulther to shoulther the brave lads keep;
Twa thousand swam ower to fell English ground,
An' danc'd themselves dry to the pibroch's sound.
Dumfounder'd, the English saw, they saw!
Dumfounder'd, they heard the blaw, the blaw!
Dumfounder'd they 'a ran awa', awa'!
Frae the hundred pipers an' a', an' a'! *(chorus)*

Carolina, Lady Nairne

UPON SAINT CRISPIN'S DAY

      HE which hath no stomach to this fight,
      Let him depart, his passport shall be made,
And crowns for convoy put into his purse;
We would not die in that man's company
That fears his fellowship to die with us.
This day is call'd the feast of Crispian.
He that outlives this day, and comes safe home,
Will stand a tip-toe when this day is nam'd,
And rouse him at the name of Crispian.
He that shall live this day, and see old age,
Will yearly on the vigil feast his neighbours,
And say 'Tomorrow is Saint Crispian.'
Then will he strip his sleeve and show his scars,
And say 'These wounds I had on Crispian's day.'
Old men forget; yet all shall be forgot,
But he'll remember, with advantages,
What feats he did that day. Then shall our names,
Familiar in his mouth as household words—
Harry the King, Bedford and Exeter,
Warwick and Talbot, Salisbury and Gloucester—
Be in their flowing cups freshly rememb'red.
This story shall the good man teach his son;
And Crispin Crispian shall ne'er go by,
From this day to the ending of the world,
But we in it shall be remembered—
We few, we happy few, we band of brothers;
For he today that sheds his blood with me
Shall be my brother; be he ne'er so vile,
This day shall gentle his condition;
And gentlemen in England now a-bed
Shall think themselves accurs'd they were not here,
And hold their manhoods cheap whiles any speaks
That fought with us upon Saint Crispin's day.

William Shakespeare, from King Henry the Fifth

AFTER BLENHEIM

'TWAS a summer evening,
  Old Kaspar's work was done,
And he before his cottage door
  Was sitting in the sun,
And by him sported on the green
His little grandchild, Wilhelmine.

She saw her brother Peterkin
  Roll something large and round,
Which he beside the rivulet
  In playing there had found;
He came to ask what he had found
That was so large, and smooth, and round.

Old Kaspar took it from the boy
  Who stood expectant by;
And then the old man shook his head
  And with a natural sigh—
"Tis some poor fellow's skull,' said he,
'Who fell in that great victory.'

'I find them in the garden,
  For there's many here about;
And often when I go to plough
  The ploughshare turns them out.
For many thousand men,' said he,
'Were slain in that great victory.'

'Now tell us what 'twas all about,'
  Young Peterkin, he cries;
And little Willhelmine looks up
  With wonder-waiting eyes;
'Now tell us all about the war,
And what they fought each other for.'

'It was the English,' Kaspar cried,
  'Who put the French to rout;
But what they fought each other for
  I could not well make out;
But everbody said,' quoth he,
'That 'twas a famous victory.

And everybody praised the Duke
   Who this great fight did win.'
'But what good came of it at last?'
   Quoth little Peterkin.
'Why, that I cannot tell,' said he,
'But 'twas a famous victory.'

Robert Southey

THE EVE OF THE BATTLE OF WATERLOO

THERE was a sound of revelry by night,
   And Belgium's capital had gather'd then
Her Beauty and her Chivalry, and bright
The lamps shone o'er fair women and brave men;
A thousand hearts beat happily; and when
Music arose with its voluptious swell,
Soft eyes look'd love to eyes which spoke again,
And all went merry as a marriage bell;
But hush! hark! a deep sound strikes like a rising knell!

Did ye not hear it?—No; 'twas but the wind,
Or the car rattling o'er the stony street;
On with the dance! let joy be unconfined;
No sleep till morn, when Youth and Pleasure meet
To chase the glowing Hours with flying feet—
But hark! that heavy sound breaks in once more,
As if the clouds its echo would repeat;
And nearer, clearer, deadlier than before!
Arm! Arm! it is—it is—the cannon's opening roar!

Within a window'd niche of that high hall
Sate Brunswick's fated chieftain; he did hear
That sound the first amid the festival,
And caught its tone with Death's prophetic ear;
And when they smiled because he deemed it near,
His heart more truly knew that peal too well
Which stretch'd his father on a bloody bier,
And roused the vengeance blood alone could quell;
He rushed into the field, and, foremost fighting, fell.

Ah! then and there was hurrying to and fro,
And gathering tears, and tremblings of distress,

And cheeks all pale, which but an hour ago
Blush'd at the praise of their own loveliness;
And there were sudden partings, such as press
The life from out young hearts, and choking sighs
Which ne'er might be repeated; who could guess
If ever more should meet those mutual eyes,
Since upon night so sweet such awful morn could rise!

And there was mounting in hot haste: the steed,
The mustering squadron, and the clattering car,
Went pouring forward with impetuous speed,
And swiftly forming in the ranks of war;
And the deep thunder peal on peal afar;
And near, the beat of the alarming drum
Roused up the soldier ere the morning star;
While throng'd the citizens with terror dumb,
Or whispering, with white lips—'The foe! they come! they come!'

George Gordon, Lord Byron from Childe Harold's Pilgrimage

SAY NOT THE STRUGGLE NAUGHT AVAILETH

SAY not the struggle naught availeth,
   The labour and the wounds are vain,
The enemy faints not, nor faileth,
   And as things have been they remain.

If hopes were dupes, fears may be liars;
   It may be, in yon smoke conceal'd,
Your comrades chase e'en now the fliers,
   And, but for you, possess the field.

For while the tired waves, vainly breaking,
   Seem here no painful inch to gain,
Far back, through creeks and inlets making,
   Comes silent flooding in, the main.

And not by eastern windows only,
   When daylight comes, comes in the light;
in front the sun climbs slow, how slowly!
   But westward, look, the land is bright!

Arthur Hugh Clough

NOVEMBER EVES

NOVEMBER Evenings! Damp and still
They used to cloak Leckhampton hill,
And lie down close on the grey plain,
And dim the dripping window-pane,
And send queer winds like Harlequins
That seized our elms for violins
And struck a note so sharp and low
Even a child could feel the woe.

Now fire chased shadow round the room,
Tables and chairs grew vast in gloom:
We crept about like mice, while Nurse
Sat mending, solemn as a hearse,
And even our unlearned eyes
Half closed with choking memories.

Is it the mist or the dead leaves,
Or the dead men— November eves?

James Elroy Flecker

THE SOLDIER

IF I should die, think only this of me:
That there's some corner of a foreign field
That is for ever England. There shall be
   In that rich earth a richer dust conceal'd;
A dust whom England bore, shaped, made aware,
   Gave, once, her flowers to love, her ways to roam,
A body of England's, breathing English air,
   Wash'd by the rivers, blest by suns of home.
And think, this heart, all evil shed away,
   A pulse in the eternal mind, no less
      Gives somewhere back the thoughts by England given;
Her sights and sounds, dreams happy as her day;
   And laughter, learnt of friends; and gentleness,
      In hearts at peace, under an English heaven.

Rupert Brooke

INTO BATTLE

THE naked earth is warm with spring,
   And with green grass and bursting trees
Leans to the sun's gaze glorying,
   And quivers in the sunny breeze;
And life is colour and warmth and light,
   And a striving evermore for these;
And he is dead who will not fight;
   And who dies fighting has increase.

The fighting man shall from the sun
   Take warmth, and life from the glowing earth;
Speed with the light-foot winds to run,
   And with the trees to newer birth;
And find, when fighting shall be done,
   Great rest, and fullness after dearth.

Julian Grenfell, an extract

ANTHEM FOR DOOMED YOUTH

WHAT passing-bells for these who die as cattle?
   Only the monstrous anger of the guns.
Only the stuttering rifles rapid rattle
Can patter out their hasty orisons.
No mockeries for them from prayers or bells,
   Nor any voice of mourning save the choirs,—
The shrill, demented choirs of wailing shells;
   And bugles calling for them from sad shires.

What candles may be held to speed them all?
   Not in the hands of boys, but in their eyes
Shall shine the holy glimmers of good-byes.
   The pallor of girls' brows shall be their pall;
Their flowers the tenderness of silent minds,
And each slow dusk a drawing-down of blinds.

Wilfrid Owen

IN FLANDERS FIELDS

IN Flanders fields the poppies blow
Between the crosses, row on row,
    That mark our place; and in the sky
    The larks, still bravely singing, fly
Scarce heard amid the guns below.

We are the Dead. Short days ago
We lived, felt dawn, saw sunset glow,
Loved and were loved, and now we lie
    In Flanders fields.

Take up our quarrel with the foe:
To you from failing hands we throw
    The torch, be yours to hold it high.
    If ye break faith with us who die
We shall not sleep, tho' poppies grow
    In Flanders fields.

John Macrae

THE DUKE OF BURGUNDY PRAISES PEACE

MY duty to you both, on equal love,
Great Kings of France and England! That I have labour'd
With all my wits, my pains, and strong endeavours,
To bring your most imperial Majesties
Upon this bar and royal interview,
Your mightiness on both parts best can witness.
Since then my office hath so far prevail'd
That face to face and royal eye to eye
You have congreeted, let it not disgrace me
If I demand, before this royal view,
What rub or what impediment there is
Why that the naked, poor, and mangled Peace,
Dear nurse of arts, plenties, and joyful births,
Should not in this best garden of the world,
Our fertile France, put up her lovely visage?
Alas, she hath from France too long been chas'd!
And all her husbandry doth lie on heaps,
Corrupting in its own fertility.
Her vine, the merry cheerer of the heart,

Unpruned dies; her hedges even-pleached,
Like prisoners wildly overgrown with hair,
Put forth disorder'd twigs; her fallow leas
The darnel, hemlock, and rank fumitory,
Doth root upon, while that the coulter rusts
That should deracinate such savagery;
The even mead, that erst brought sweetly forth
The freckled cowslip, burnet, and green clover,
Wanting the scythe, all uncorrected, rank,
Conceives by idleness, and nothing teems
But hateful docks, rough thistles, kecksies, burs,
Losing both beauty and utility.
And as our vineyards, fallows, meads, and hedges,
Defective in their natures, grow to wildness;
Even so our houses and ourselves and children
Have lost, or do not learn for want of time,
The sciences that should become our country;
But grow, like savages—as soldiers will,
That nothing do but meditate on blood—
To swearing and stern looks, diffus'd attire,
And everything that seems unnatural.
Which to reduce into our former favour
You are assembled; and my speech entreats
That I may know the let why gentle Peace
Should not expel these inconveniences
And bless us with her former qualities.

William Shakespeare, from King Henry the Fifth

THE HORNS OF
ELFLAND
FAINTLY BLOWING

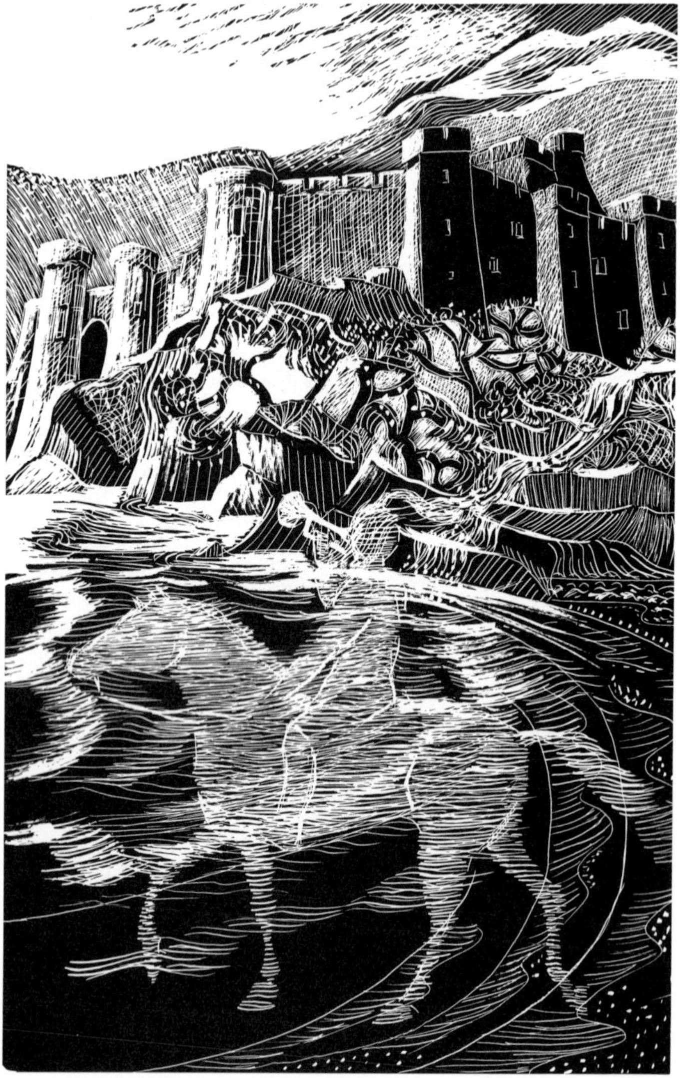

ARIEL'S SONG

WHERE the bee sucks, there suck I;
  In a cowslip's bell I lie;
There I couch when owls do cry.
On the bat's back I do fly
After summer merrily.
Merrily, merrily shall I live now
Under the blossom that hangs on the bough.

William Shakespeare, from The Tempest

BLOW, BUGLE, BLOW

THE splendour falls on castle walls
  And snowy summits old in story;
The long light shakes across the lakes,
  And the wild cataract leaps in glory.
Blow, bugle, blow, set the wild echoes flying,
Blow bugle; answer, echoes, dying, dying, dying.

O hark, O hear! how thin and clear,
  And thinner, clearer, farther going!
O sweet and far from cliff and scar
  The horns of Elfland faintly blowing!
Blow, let us hear the purple glens replying;
Blow, bugle; answer, echoes, dying, dying, dying.

O love, they die in yon rich sky,
  They faint on hill or field or river;
Our echoes roll from soul to soul,
  And grow for ever and for ever.
Blow, bugle, blow, set the wild echoes flying,
And answer, echoes, answer, dying, dying, dying.

Alfred, Lord Tennyson, from The Princess

TITANIA'S ORDERS

Come now, a roundel and a fairy song;
  Then, for the third part of a minute, hence:
Some to kill cankers in the musk-rose buds;
Some, war with rere-mice for their leathern wings,
To make my small elves coats; and some keep back

The clamorous owl that nightly hoots and wonders
At our quaint spirits.

    William Shakespeare, from A Midsummer Night's Dream

KUBLA KHAN

IN Xanadu did Kubla Khan
A stately pleasure-dome decree:
Where Alph, the sacred river, ran
Through caverns measureless to man
    Down to a sunless sea.
So twice five miles of fertile ground
With walls and towers were girdled round:
And here were gardens bright with sinuous rills,
Where blossomed many an incense-bearing tree;
And here were forests ancient as the hills,
Enfolding sunny spots of greenery.

But oh! that deep romantic chasm which slanted
Down the green hill athwart a cedarn cover!
A savage place! as holy and enchanted
As e'er beneath a waning moon was haunted
By woman wailing for her demon-lover!
And from this chasm, with ceaseless turmoil seething,
As if this earth in fast thick pants were breathing,
A mighty fountain momently was forced:
Amid whose swift half-intermitted burst
Huge fragments vaulted like rebounding hail,
Or chaffy grain beneath the thresher's flail:
And 'mid these dancing rocks at once and ever
It flung up momently the sacred river.
Five miles meandering with a mazy motion
Through wood and dale the sacred river ran,
Then reached the caverns measureless to man,
And sank in tumult to a lifeless ocean:
And 'mid this tumult Kubla heard from far
Ancestral voices prophesying war!
    The shadow of the dome of pleasure
      Floated midway on the waves;
    Where was heard the mingled measure
      From the fountain and the caves.

It was a miracle of rare device,
A sunny pleasure-dome with caves of ice!

   A damsel with a dulcimer
   In a vision once I saw:
   It was an Abyssinian maid,
   And on her dulcimer she played,
   Singing of Mount Abora.
   Could I revive within me
   Her symphony and song,
   To such a deep delight 'twould win me,
That with music loud and long,
I would build that dome in air,
That sunny dome! those caves of ice!
And all who heard should see them there,
And all should cry, Beware! Beware!
His flashing eyes, his floating hair!
Weave a circle round him thrice,
And close your eyes with holy dread,
For he on honey-dew hath fed,
And drunk the milk of Paradise.

Samuel Taylor Coleridge

ON FIRST LOOKING INTO CHAPMAN'S HOMER

MUCH had I travell'd in the realms of gold,
   And many goodly states and kingdoms seen;
   Round many western islands have I been
Which bards in fealty to Apollo hold.
Oft of one wide expanse had I been told
   That deep-brow'd Homer ruled as his demesne;
   Yet did I never breathe its pure serene
Till I heard Chapman speak out loud and bold:
Then felt I like some watcher of the skies
   When a new planet swims into his ken;
Or like stout Cortes when with eagle eyes
   He stared at the Pacific—and all his men
Look'd at each other with a wild surmise—
   Silent, upon a peak in Darien.

John Keats

THE DEMON LOVER

'O WHERE have you been, my long, long, love,
  This long seven years and more?'
'O I'm come to seek my former vows
  Ye granted me before.'

'O hold your tongue of your former vows,
  For they will breed sad strife;
O hold your tongue of your former vows,
  For I am become a wife.'

He turned him right and round about,
  And the tear blinded his ee;
'I would never have trodden on Irish ground,
  If it had not been for thee.

I might have had a king's daughter,
  Far, far beyond the sea;
I might have had a king's daughter,
  Had it not been for love of thee.'

'If ye might have had a king's daughter,
  Yourself you had to blame;
Ye might have taken the king's daughter,
  For ye knew that I was nane.'

'O false are the vows of womankind,
  But fair is their false bodie;
I never would have trodden on Irish ground
  Had it not been for love of thee.'

'If I were to leave my husband dear,
  And my two babes also,
O what have you to take me to,
  If with you I should go?'

'I have seven ships upon the sea,
  The eighth brought me to land;
With four and twenty bold mariners,
  And music on every hand.'

She has taken up her two little babes,
  Kiss'd them both cheek and chin;

'O fare ye well, my own two babes,
  For I'll never see you again.'

She set her foot upon the ship,
  No mariners could she behold;
But the sails were of taffetie,
  And the masts of beaten gold.

She had not sail'd a league, a league,
  A league but barely three,
When dismal grew his countenance,
  And drumlie grew his ee.

The masts that were like beaten gold
  Bent not on the heaving seas;
And the sails that were of taffetie
  Fill'd not in the east land breeze.

They had not sail'd a league, a league,
  A league but barely three,
Until she spied his cloven foot,
  And she wept right bitterly.

'O hold your tongue of your weeping,' says he,
  'Of your weeping now let me be;
I will show you how the lilies grow
  On the banks of Italy.'

'O what hills are yon, yon pleasant hills,
  That the sun shines sweetly on?'
'O yon are the hills of heaven,' he said,
  'Where you will never won.'

'O what a mountain is yon,' she said,
  'All so dreary with frost and snow?'
'O yon is the mountain of hell,' he cried,
  'Where you and I will go.'

And aye when she turn'd her round about
  Aye taller he seem'd for to be;
Until that the tops of that gallant ship
  No taller were than he.

The clouds grew dark and the wind grew loud,
    And the levin filled her ee;
And waesome wail'd the snow-white sprites
    Upon the gurlie sea.

He struck the topmast with his hand,
    The foremast with his knee;
And he break that gallant ship in twain,
    And sank her in the sea.

Old Ballad

LA BELLE DAME SANS MERCI

AH, what can ail thee, Knight at arms,
    Alone and palely loitering?
The sedge is wither'd from the lake,
    And no birds sing.

Ah, what can ail thee, Knight at arms,
    So haggard and so woe-begone?
The squirrel's granary is full,
    And the harvest's done.

I see a lily on thy brow,
    With anguish moist and fever dew;
And on thy cheek a fading rose
    Fast withereth too.

I met a lady in the meads,
    Full beautiful, a faery's child;
Her hair was long, her foot was light,
    And her eyes were wild.

I set her on my pacing steed,
    And nothing else saw all day long;
For sideways would she lean, and sing
    A faery's song.

I made a garland for her head,
    And bracelets too, and fragrant zone;
She look'd at me as she did love,
    And made sweet moan.

She found me roots of relish sweet,
  And honey wild, and manna dew;
And sure in language strange she said,
  I love thee true.

She took me to her elfin grot,
  And there she gaz'd and sighed deep,
And there I shut her wild sad eyes—
  So kiss'd to sleep.

And there we slumber'd on the moss,
  And there I dream'd, ah woe betide,
The latest dream I ever dream'd
  On the cold hill side.

I saw pale kings, and princes too,
  Pale warriors, death-pale were they all;
Who cried 'La belle Dame sans merci
  Hath thee in thrall!'

I saw their starv'd lips in the gloam
  With horrid warning gaped wide,
And I awoke, and found me here,
  On the cold hill side.

And this is why I sojourn here
  Alone and palely loitering,
Though the sedge is wither'd from the lake,
  And no birds sing.

John Keats

SCARBOROUGH FAIR

'*O where are you going?' 'To Scarborough fair.'*
  Parsley, sage, rosemary and thyme.
'*Remember me to a lass that lives there;*
  For once she was a true lover of mine.'

'And tell her to make me a cambric shirt,
  Without a needle or thread or ought else;
And tell her to wash it in yonder well,
  Where ne'er sprung water nor a drop of rain fell;
And tell her to hang it on yonder stone,

    Where moss never grew since Adam was born,
And when she has finished and done, I'll repay,
    She can come with me and married we'll be.'

'O where are you going?' 'To Scarborough fair.'
Parsley, sage, rosemary and thyme.
'Remember me to a lad who lives there;
    For once he was a true lover of mine.'

'And tell him to buy me an acre of land,
    Between the wide ocean and the sea-sand;
And tell him to plow it with a ram's horn,
    And sow it all over with one pepper-corn.
And tell him to reap 't with a sickle of leather,
    And bind it up with a peacock's feather.
And when he has finished, and done his work,
    He can come unto me for his cambric shirt.'

Old Ballad—A Version of The Elfin Knight

QUEEN MAB

O, THEN I see Queen Mab hath been with you.
    She is the fairies' midwife, and she comes
In shape no bigger than an agate stone
On the fore-finger of an alderman,
Drawn with a team of little atomies
Athwart men's noses as they lie asleep;
Her wagon-spokes made of long spinners' legs;
The cover, of the wings of grasshoppers;
Her traces, of the smallest spider's web;
Her collars, of the moonshine's wat'ry beams;
Her whip, of cricket's bone; the lash, of film;
Her waggoner, a small grey-coated gnat,
Not half so big as a round little worm
Prick'd from the lazy finger of a maid.
Her chariot is an empty hazel-nut,
Made by the joiner squirrel or old grub,
Time out o' mind the fairies' coachmakers.
And in this state she gallops night by night
Through lovers' brains, and then they dream of love;
O'er courtiers' knees, that dream on curtsies straight;
O'er lawyers' fingers, who straight dream on fees;

O'er ladies' lips, who straight on kisses dream,
Which oft the angry Mab with blisters plagues,
Because their breaths with sweetmeats tainted are.
Sometime she gallops o'er a courtier's nose,
And then dreams he of smelling out a suit;
And sometime comes she with a tithe-pig's tail,
Tickling a parson's nose as 'a lies asleep,
Then dreams he of another benefice.
Sometime she driveth o'er a soldier's neck,
And then dreams he of cutting foreign throats,
Of breaches, ambuscadoes, Spanish blades,
Of healths five fathom deep; and then anon
Drums in his ear, at which he starts and wakes,
And, being thus frighted, swears a prayer or two,
And sleeps again.

William Shakespeare, from Romeo and Juliet

THE WITCHES' CAULDRON

THRICE the brinded cat hath mew'd.
Thrice and once the hedge-pig whin'd.
Harpier cries; 'tis time, 'tis time.

Round about the cauldron go;
In the poison'd entrails throw.
Toad, that under cold stone
Days and nights has thirty-one
Swelter'd venom sleeping got
Boil thou first i' th' charmed pot.

    Double, double toil and trouble;
    Fire burn, and cauldron bubble.

Fillet of a fenny snake,
In the cauldron boil and bake;
Eye of newt, and toe of frog,
Wool of bat, and tongue of dog,
Adder's fork, and blind-worm's sting,
Lizard's leg, and howlet's wing—
For a charm of pow'rful trouble,
Like a hell-broth boil and bubble.

Double, double, toil and trouble;
Fire burn, and cauldron bubble.

Scale of dragon, tooth of wolf,
Witch's mummy, maw and gulf
Of the ravin'd salt-sea shark,
Root of hemlock, digg'd i' th' dark,
Liver of blaspheming Jew,
Gall of goat, and slips of yew
Sliver'd in the moon's eclipse,
Nose of Turk, and Tartar's lips,
Finger of birth-strangled babe
Ditch-deliver'd by a drab—
Make the gruel thick and slab;
Add thereto a tiger's chaudron,
For th' ingredient of our cauldron.

Double, double, toil and trouble;
Fire burn, and cauldron bubble.

Cool it with a baboon's blood,
Then the charm is firm and good.

William Shakespeare, from Macbeth

THE DEVIL'S NINE QUESTIONS

THERE was a lady in the West.
   Lay the bank with the bonny broom!
She had three daughters of the best.
   Fa lang the dillo, dillo, dee.

There came a stranger to the gate,
And he three days and nights did wait.
The eldest daughter did ope the door,
The second set him on the floor.
The third daughter she brought a chair,
And placed it that he might sit there.

'Now answer me these questions nine,
Or you shall surely all be mine.

What is greener than the grass?
What is smoother than crystal glass?

What is brighter than the light?
What is darker than the night?

What is heavier than the lead?
What is better than the bread?

What is higher than a tree?
What is deeper than the sea?

What is rounder than a ring?'
'To you we thus our answers bring:

Envy is greener than the grass;
Flattery smoother than crystal glass.

Truth is brighter than the light;
Falsehood's darker than the night.

Sin is heavier than the lead;
The blessings better than the bread.

Heaven is higher than a tree;
Hell is deeper than the sea.

The world is rounder than a ring.
To you we thus our answers bring.
Thus you have our answers nine,
And we *never* shall be thine!'

Old Ballad

THE LADY OF SHALOTT

PART I

ON either side the river lie
Long fields of barley and of rye,
That clothe the wold and meet the sky;
And thro' the field the road runs by
      To many-tower'd Camelot;
And up and down the people go,
Gazing where the lilies blow
Round an island there below,
      The island of Shalott.

Willows whiten, aspens quiver,
Little breezes dusk and shiver
Thro' the wave that runs for ever
By the island in the river
        Flowing down to Camelot.
Four gray walls, and four gray towers,
Overlook a space of flowers,
And the silent isle imbowers
        The Lady of Shalott.

By the margin, willow-veil'd,
Slide the heavy barges trail'd
By slow horses; and unhail'd
The shallop flitteth silken-sail'd
        Skimming down to Camelot.
But who hath seen her wave her hand?
Or at the casement seen her stand?
Or is she known in all the land,
        The Lady of Shalott?

Only reapers, reaping early
In among the bearded barley,
Hear a song that echoes cheerly
From the river winding clearly,
        Down to tower'd Camelot:
And by moon the reaper weary,
Piling sheaves in uplands airy,
Listening, whispers ' 'Tis the fairy
        Lady of Shalott.'

PART II

There she weaves by night and day
A magic web with colours gay.
She has heard a whisper say,
A curse is on her if she stay
        To look down to Camelot.
She knows what the curse may be,
And so she weaveth steadily,
And little other care hath she,
        The Lady of Shalott.

And moving thro' a mirror clear
That hangs before her all the year,
Shadows of the world appear.
There she sees the highway near
        Winding down to Camelot.
There the river eddy whirls,
And there the surly village-churls,
And the red cloaks of market girls,
        Pass onward from Shalott.

Sometimes a troop of damsels glad,
An abbot on an ambling pad,
Sometimes a curly shepherd-lad,
Or long-hair'd page in crimson clad,
        Goes by to tower'd Camelot;
And sometimes thro' the mirror blue
The knights come riding two and two:
She hath no loyal knight and true,
        The Lady of Shalott.

But in her web she still delights
To weave the mirror's magic sights,
For often thro' the silent nights
A funeral, with plumes and lights
        And music, went to Camelot:
Or when the moon was overhead,
Came two young lovers lately wed;
'I am half sick of shadows,' she said
        The Lady of Shalott.

PART III

A bow-shot from her bower-eaves,
He rode between the barley-sheaves,
The sun came dazzling thro' the leaves,
And flamed upon the brazen greaves
        Of bold Sir Lancelot.
A red-cross knight for ever kneel'd
To a lady in his shield,
That sparkled on the yellow field,
        Beside remote Shalott.

The gemmy bridle glitter'd free,
Like to some branch of stars we see
Hung in the golden Galaxy.
The bridle bells rang merrily
    As he rode down to Camelot:
And from his blazon'd baldrick slung
A mighty silver bugle hung,
And as he rode his armour rung,
    Beside remote Shalott.

All in the blue unclouded weather
Thick-jewell'd shone the saddle-leather,
The helmet and the helmet-feather
Burn'd like one burning flame together,
    As he rode down to Camelot,
As often thro' the purple night,
Below the starry clusters bright,
Some bearded meteor, trailing light,
    Moves over still Shalott.

His broad clear brow in sunlight glow'd;
On burnish'd hooves his war-horse trode;
From underneath his helmet flow'd
His coal-black curls as on he rode.
    As he road down to Camelot.
From the bank and from the river
He flash'd into the crystal mirror,
'Tirra lirra,' by the river
    Sang Sir Lancelot.

She left the web, she left the loom,
She made three paces thro' the room,
She saw the water-lily bloom,
She saw the helmet and the plume,
    She look'd down to Camelot.
Out flew the web and floated wide;
The mirror crack'd from side to side;
'The curse is come upon me!' cried
    The Lady of Shalott.

THE HORNS OF ELFLAND

PART IV

In the stormy east-wind straining,
The pale yellow woods were waning,
The broad stream in his banks complaining,
Heavily the low sky raining
   Over tower'd Camelot.
Down she came and found a boat
Beneath a willow left afloat,
And round about the prow she wrote
   The Lady of Shalott.

And down the river's dim expanse
Like some bold seër in a trance,
Seeing all his own mischance—
With a glassy countenance
   Did she look to Camelot.
And at the closing of the day
She loosed the chain, and down she lay;
The broad stream bore her far away,
   The Lady of Shalott.

Lying, robed in snowy white
That loosely flew to left and right—
The leaves upon her falling light—
Thro' the noises of the night
   She floated down to Camelot:
And as the boat-head wound along
The willowy hills and fields among,
They hear her singing her last song,
   The Lady of Shalott.

Heard a carol, mournful, holy,
Chanted loudly, chanted lowly,
Till her blood was frozen slowly,
And her eyes were darkened wholly,
   Turn'd to tower'd Camelot;
For ere she reach'd upon the tide
The first house by the water-side,
Singing in her song she died,
   The Lady of Shalott.

Under tower and balcony,
By garden wall and gallery,
A gleaming shape she floated by,
Dead-pale between the houses high,
    Silent in Camelot.
Out on the wharfs they came,
Knight and burgher, lord and dame,
And round the prow they read her name,
    The Lady of Shalott.

Who is this? and what is here?
And in the lighted palace near
Died the sound of royal cheer;
And they cross'd themselves for fear,
    All the knights at Camelot:
But Lancelot mused a little space;
He said, 'She has a lovely face;
God in His mercy lend her grace,
    The Lady of Shalott.'

Alfred, Lord Tennyson

LORD RANDAL

'O, WHERE have ye been, Lord Randal, my son?
O, where have ye been, my handsome young man?'
'I have been to the wood; mother, make my bed soon,
For I'm weary with hunting, and fain would lie down.'

'Where got ye your dinner, Lord Randal, my son?
Where got ye your dinner, my handsome young man?'
'I dined with my love; mother make my bed soon,
For I'm weary with hunting, and fain would lie down.'

'What got ye to dinner, Lord Randal, my son?
What got ye to dinner, my handsome young man?'
'I got eels boil'd in broth; mother, make my bed soon,
For I'm weary with hunting, and fain would lie down.'

'And where are your bloodhounds, Lord Randal, my son?
And where are your bloodhounds, my handsome young man?'
'O, they swell'd and they died; mother, make my bed soon,
For I'm weary with hunting, and fain would lie down.'

'O, I fear ye are poison'd, Lord Randal, my son!
O, I fear ye are poisoned, my handsome young man!'
'O, yes, I am poison'd! mother, make my bed soon,
For I'm sick at the heart, and I fain would lie down.'

Old Ballad

THE FAIRY QUEEN'S BED

I KNOW a bank where the wild thyme blows,
Where oxlips and the nodding violet grows,
Quite over-canopied with luscious woodbine,
With sweet musk-roses, and with eglantine;
There sleeps Titania sometime of the night,
Lull'd in these flowers with dances and delight;
And there the snake throws her enamell'd skin,
Weed wide enough to wrap a fairy in…

William Shakespeare, from A Midsummer Night's Dream

PUCK DECRIBES THE FAIRIES' FAVOURITE TIME

NOW the hungry lion roars,
And the wolf behowls the moon;
Whilst the heavy ploughman snores,
All with weary task fordone.
Now the wasted brands do glow,
Whilst the screech-owl, screeching loud,
Puts the wretch that lies in woe
In remembrance of a shroud.
Now it is the time of night
That the graves, all gaping wide,
Every one lets forth his sprite,
In the church-way paths to glide.
And we fairies, that do run
By the triple Hecate's team
From the presence of the sun,
Following darkness like a dream,
Now are frolic. Not a mouse
Shall disturb this house.
I am sent with broom before,
To sweep the dust behind the door.

William Shakespeare, from A Midsummer Night's Dream

THE FAIRIES' FAREWELL

'FAREWELL, rewards and fairies.'
   Good housewives now may say,
For now foul sluts in dairies
   Do fare as well as they.
And though they sweep their hearths no less
   Than maids were wont to do,
Yet who of late, for cleanliness,
   Finds sixpence in her shoe?...

At morning and in evening both
   You merry were and glad;
So little care of sleep or sloth
   These pretty ladies had;
When Tom came home from labour,
   Or Ciss to milking rose,
Then merrily merrily went their tabour
   And nimbly went their toes.

Witness those rings and roundelays
   Of theirs, which yet remain,
Were footed in Queen Mary's days
   On many a grassy plain;
But since of late, Elizabeth,
   And later James came in,
They never danced on any heath
   As when the time hath been.

Richard Corbett

PUT ON THE WHOLE ARMOUR

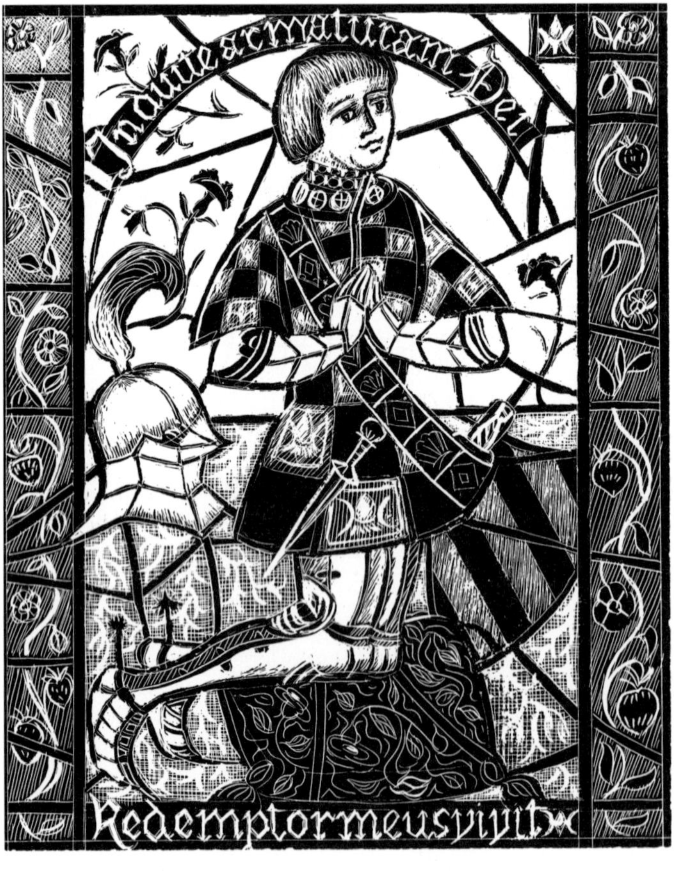
Induite armaturam Dei
Redemptor meus vivit

THE KNIGHT

A KNIGHT ther was, and that a worthy man,
That fro the tyme that he first bigan
To ryden out, he loved chivalrye,
Trouthe and honour, fredom and curteisye.
Ful worthy was he in his lordes werre,
And therto hadde he riden (no man ferre)
As wel in Cristendom as hethenesse,
And ever honoured for his worthinesse....
At mortal batailles hadde he been fiftene,
And foughten for our feith at Tramissene
In listes thryes, and ay slayn his fo.
This ilke worthy knight had been also
Somtyme with the lord of Palatye,
Ageyn another hethen in Turkye:
And evermore he hadde a sovereyn prys.
And though that he were worthy, he was wys,
And of his port as meke as is a mayde.
He never yet no vileinye ne sayde,
In al his lyf, un-to no maner wight,
He was a verray parfit, gentil knight.

Geoffrey Chaucer, from The Prologue to The Canterbury Tales

MERCY

THE quality of mercy is not strain'd;
It droppeth as the gentle rain from heaven
Upon the place beneath. It is twice blest:
It blesseth him that gives and him that takes.
'Tis mightiest in the mightiest; it becomes
The throned monarch better than his crown;
His sceptre shows the force of temporal power,
The attribute to awe and majesty,
Wherein doth sit the dread and fear of kings;
But mercy is above this sceptred sway,
It is enthroned in the heart of kings,
It is an attribute to God himself;
And earthly power doth then show likest God's
When mercy seasons justice.

William Shakespeare, from The Merchant of Venice

JUSTICE

THE rain it raineth on the just
And also on the unjust fella:
But chiefly on the just, because
   The unjust steals the just's umbrella.

Charles, Lord Bowen, from Sichel, Sands of Time

ORDER

AND look how many Grecian tents do stand
. . . Hollow upon this plain, so many hollow factions.
When that the general is not like the hive,
To whom the foragers shall all repair,
What honey is expected? Degree being vizarded,
Th' unworthiest shows as fairly in the mask.
The heavens themselves, the planets, and this centre,
Observe degree, priority, and place,
Insisture, course, proportion, season, form,
Office, and custom, in all line of order;
And therefore is the glorious planet Sol
In noble eminence enthron'd and spher'd
Amidst the other, whose med'cinable eye
Corrects the ill aspects of planets evil,
And posts, like the commandment of a king,
Sans check, to good and bad. But when the planets
In evil mixture to disorder wander,
What plagues and what portents, what mutiny,
What raging of the sea, shaking of earth,
Commotion in the winds! Frights, changes, horrors,
Divert and crack, rend and deracinate,
The unity and married calm of states
Quite from their fixture! O, when degree is shak'd,
Which is the ladder of all high designs,
The enterprise is sick! How could communities,
Degrees in schools, and brotherhoods in cities,
Peaceful commerce from dividable shores,
The primogenity and due of birth,
Prerogative of age, crowns, sceptres, laurels,
But by degree, stand in authentic place?
Take but degree away, untune that string,
And hark what discord follows! Each thing melts

In mere oppugnancy: the bounded waters
Should lift their bosoms higher than the shores,
And make a sop of all this solid globe;
Strength should be lord of imbecility,
And the rude son should strike his father dead;
Force should be right; or, rather, right and wrong—
Between whose endless jar justice resides—
Should lose their names, and so should justice too.
Then everything includes itself in power,
Power into will, will into appetite;
And appetite, an universal wolf,
So doubly seconded with will and power,
Must make perforce an universal prey,
And last eat up himself. Great Agamemnon,
This chaos, when degree is suffocate,
Follows the choking.
And this neglection of degree it is
That by a pace goes backward, with a purpose
It hath to climb. The general's disdain'd
By him one step below, he by the next,
That next by him beneath; so every step,
Exampl'd by the first pace that is sick
Of his superior, grows to an envious fever
Of pale and bloodless emulation.

William Shakespeare, from Troilus and Cressida

THE PIED PIPER OF HAMELIN

A CHILD'S STORY

HAMELIN Town's in Brunswick,
By famous Hanover city;
The river Weser, deep and wide,
Washes its wall on the southern side;
A pleasanter spot you never spied;
   But, when begins my ditty,
Almost five hundred years ago,
To see the townsfolk suffer so
   From vermin, was a pity.

Rats!
They fought the dogs and killed the cats,
    And bit the babies in the cradles,
And ate the cheeses out of the vats,
    And licked the soup from the cooks' own ladles,
Split open the kegs of salted sprats,
Made nests inside men's Sunday hats,
And even spoiled the women's chats
       By drowning their speaking
       With shrieking and squeaking
In fifteen different sharps and flats.

At last the people in a body
    To the Town Hall came flocking:
' 'Tis clear,' cried they, 'our Mayor's a noddy;
    And as for our Corporation—shocking—
To think we buy gowns lined with ermine
For dolts that can't or won't determine
What's best to rid us of our vermin!
You hope, because you're old and obese,
To find in the furry civic robes ease?
Rouse up, sirs! Give your brains a racking
To find the remedy we're lacking,
Or, sure as fate, we'll send you packing!'
At this the Mayor and Corporation
Quaked with a mighty consternation.

An hour they sat in council,
    At length the Mayor broke silence:
'For a guilder I'd my ermine gown sell,
    I wish I were a mile hence!
It's easy to bid one rack one's brain—
I'm sure my poor head aches again,
I've scratched it so, and all in vain.
Oh for a trap, a trap, a trap!'
Just as he said this, what should hap
At the chamber door but a gentle tap?
'Bless us,' cried the Mayor, 'What's that?'
(With the Corporation as he sat,
Looking little though wondrous fat;
Nor brighter was his eye, nor moister
Than a too-long-opened oyster,

Save when at noon his paunch grew mutinous
For a plate of turtle green and glutinous)
'Only a scraping of shoes on the mat?
Anything like the sound of a rat
Makes my heart go pit-a-pat!'

'Come in!' the Mayor cried, looking bigger:
And in did come the strangest figure!
His queer long coat from heel to head
Was half of yellow and half of red,
And he himself was tall and thin,
With sharp blue eyes, each like a pin,
And light loose hair, yet swarthy skin,
No tuft on cheek nor beard on chin,
But lips where smiles went out and in;
There was no guessing his kith and kin:
And nobody could enough admire
The tall man and his quaint attire.
Quoth one: 'It's as my great-grandsire,
Starting up at the Trump of Doom's tone,
Had walked this way from his painted tombstone!'

He advanced to the council-table:
And, 'Please your honours,' said he, 'I'm able
By means of a secret charm, to draw
   All creatures living beneath the sun,
   That creep or swim or fly or run,
After me so as you never saw!
And I chiefly use my charm
On creatures that do people harm,
The mole and toad and newt and viper;
And people call me the Pied Piper.'
(And here they noticed round his neck
   A scarf of red and yellow stripe,
To match his coat of the self-same cheque;
   And at the scarf's end hung a pipe;
And his fingers, they noticed, were ever straying
As if impatient to be playing
Upon this pipe, as low it dangled
Over his vesture so old-fangled.)
'Yet,' said he, 'poor piper as I am,
In Tartary I freed the Cham,

Last June, from his huge swarms of gnats;
I eased in Asia the Nizam
    Of a monstrous brood of vampyre-bats:
And as for what your brain bewilders,
    If I can rid your town of rats
Will you give me a thousand guilders?'
'One? fifty thousand!'—was the exclamation
Of the astonished Mayor and Corporation.

Into the street the Piper stept,
    Smiling first a little smile,
As if he knew what magic slept
    In his quiet pipe the while;
Then, like a musical adept,
To blow the pipe his lips he wrinkled,
And green and blue his sharp eyes twinkled,
Like a candle-flame where salt is sprinkled;
And ere three shrill notes the pipe uttered,
You heard as if an army muttered;
And the muttering grew to a grumbling;
And the grumbling grew to a mighty rumbling;
And out of the houses the rats came tumbling.
Great rats, small rats, leans rats, brawny rats,
Brown rats, black rats, grey rats, tawny rats,
Grave old plodders, gay young friskers,
    Fathers, mothers, uncles, cousins,
Cocking tails and pricking whiskers,
    Families by tens and dozens,
Brothers, sisters, husbands, wives—
Followed the Piper for their lives.
From street to street he piped advancing,
And step by step they followed dancing,
Unitl they came to the river Weser,
    Wherein all plunged and perished!
    Save one who, stout as Julius Caesar,
Swam across and lived to carry
    (As he, the manuscript he cherished)
To Rat-land home his commentary:
Which was, 'At the first shrill notes of the pipe,
I heard a sound of scraping tripe,
And putting apples, wondrous ripe,

Into a cider-press's gripe:
And a moving away of pickle-tub-boards,
And a leaving ajar of conserve-cupboards,
And a drawing the corks of train-oil-flasks,
And a breaking the hoops of butter-casks:
And it seemed as if a voice
   (Sweeter far than by harp or by psaltery
Is breathed) called out, "Oh rats, rejoice!
   The world is grown to one vast dry-saltery!
So munch on, crunch on, take your nuncheon,
Breakfast, supper, dinner, luncheon!"
'And just as a bulky sugar-puncheon,
All ready staved, like a great sun shone
Glorious scarce an inch before me,
Just as methought it said, "Come, bore me!"
—I found the Weser rolling o'er me.'

You should have heard the Hamelin people
Ringing the bells till they rocked the steeple.
'Go,' cried the Mayor, 'and get long poles,
Poke out the nests and block up the holes!
Consult with carpenters and builders,
And leave in our town not a trace
Of the rats!'—when suddenly, up the face
Of the Piper perked in the market-place,
With a, 'First, if you please, my thousand guilders!'

A thousand guilders! The Mayor looked blue;
So did the Corporation too.
For council dinners made rare havoc
With Claret, Moselle, Vin-de-Grave, Hock;
And half the money would replenish
Their cellars biggest butt with Rhenish.
To pay this sum to a wandering fellow
With a gypsy coat of red and yellow!
'Beside,' quoth the Mayor with a knowing wink,
'Our business was done at the river's brink;
We saw with our eyes the vermin sink,
And what's dead can't come to life, I think.
So, friend, we're not the folks to shrink
From the duty of giving you something for drink,
And a matter of money to put in your poke;

But as for the guilders, what we spoke
Of them, as you very well know, was in joke.
Beside, our losses have made us thrifty.
A thousand guilders! Come, take fifty!'

The Piper's face fell, and he cried
'No trifling! I can't wait, beside!
I've promised to visit by dinnertime
Bagdat, and accept the prime
Of the head-cook's pottage, all he's rich in,
For having left in the Caliph's kitchen,
Of a nest of scorpions, no survivor.
With him I proved no bargain-driver,
With you, don't think I'll bate a stiver!
And folks who put me in a passion
May find me pipe to another fashion.'
'How?' cried the Mayor, 'd'ye think I brook
Being worse treated than a Cook?
Insulted by a lazy ribald
With idle pipe and vesture piebald?
You threaten us, fellow? Do your worst,
Blow your pipe there till you burst!'

Once more he stept into the street,
   And to his lips again
   Laid his long pipe of smooth straight cane;
And ere he blew three notes (such sweet
Soft notes as yet musician's cunning
   Never gave the enraptured air)
There was a rustling that seemed like a bustling
Of merry crowds justling at pitching and hustling,
Small feet were pattering, wooden shoes clattering,
Little hands clapping and little tongues chattering,
And, like fowls in a farm-yard when barley is scattering,
Out came the children running.
All the little boys and girls,
With rosy cheeks and flaxen curls,
And sparkling eyes and teeth like pearls,
Tripping and skipping, ran merrily after
The wonderful music with shouting and laughter.

The Mayor was dumb, and the Council stood
As if they were changed into blocks of wood,
Unable to move a step, or cry
To the children merrily skipping by,
—Could only follow with the eye
That joyous crowd at the Piper's back.
But how the Mayor was on the rack,
And the wretched Council's bosoms beat,
As the Piper turned from the High Street
To where the Weser rolled its waters
Right in the way of their sons and daughters!
However he turned from South to West,
And to Koppelberg Hill his steps addressed,
And after him the children pressed;
Great was the joy in every breast.
'He never can cross that mighty top!
He's forced to let the piping drop!
And we shall see our children stop!'
When, lo, as they reached the mountain-side,
A wondrous portal opened wide,
As if a cavern was suddenly hollowed;
And the Piper advanced and the children followed,
And when all were in to the very last,
The door in the mountain-side shut fast.
Did I say, all? No! One was lame,
    And could not dance the whole of the way;
And in after years, if you would blame
    His sadness, he was used to say,—
'It's dull in our town since my playmates left!
I can't forget that I'm bereft
Of all the pleasant sights they see,
Which the Piper also promised me.
For he led us, he said, to a joyous land,
Joining the town and just at hand,
Where waters gushed and fruit-trees grew
And flowers put forth a fairer hue,
And everything was strange and new;
The sparrows were brighter than peacocks here,
And their dogs outran our fallow deer,
And the honey-bees had lost their stings,
And horses were born with eagles' wings:

And just as I became assured
My lame foot would be speedily cured,
The music stopped and I stood still,
And found myself outside the hill,
Left alone against my will,
To go now limping as before,
And never hear of that country more!'

Alas, alas for Hamelin!
    There came into many a burgher's pate
    A text which says that heaven's gate
    Opes to the rich at as easy rate
As the needle's eye takes a camel in!
The Mayor sent East, West, North and South,
To offer the Piper, by word of mouth,
    Wherever it was men's lot to find him,
Silver and gold to his heart's content,
If he'd only return the way he went,
    And bring the children behind him.
But when they saw 'twas a lost endeavour,
And Piper and dancers were gone for ever,
They made a decree that lawyers never
    Should think their records dated duly
If, after the day of the month and year,
These words did not as well appear,
'And so long after what happened here
    On the Twenty-second of July,
Thirteen hundred and seventy-six:'
And the better in memory to fix
The place of the children's last retreat,
They called it, the Pied Piper's Street—
Where anyone playing on pipe or tabor
Was sure for the future to lose his labour,
Nor suffered they hostelry or tavern
    To shock with mirth a street so solemn;
But opposite the place of the cavern
    They wrote the story on a column,
And on the great church-window painted
The same, to make the world acquainted
How their children were stolen away,
And there it stands to this very day.

And I must not omit to say
That in Transylvania there's a tribe
Of alien people who ascribe
The outlandish ways and dress
On which their neighbours lay such stress,
To their fathers and mothers having risen
Out of some subterraneous prison
Into which they were trepanned
Long time ago in a mighty band
Out of Hamelin town in Brunswick land,
But how or why, they don't understand,

So, Willy, let me and you be wipers
Of scores out with all men—especially pipers!
And, whether they pipe us free fróm rats or fróm mice,
If we've promised them aught, let us keep our promise!

Robert Browning

THE ANT AND THE CRICKET

A SILLY young Cricket, accustomed to sing
Through the warm, sunny months of gay summer and spring,
Began to complain, when he found that at home
His cupboard was empty and winter was come.
      Not a crumb to be found
      On the snow-covered ground;
      Not a flower could he see,
      Not a leaf on a tree;
'Oh, what will become,' says the Cricket, 'of me?'

At last by starvation and famine made bold,
All dripping with wet and trembling with cold,
Away he set off to a miserly Ant,
To see if, to keep him alive, he would grant
      Him shelter from rain:
      A mouthful of grain—
      He wished only to borrow,
      He'd repay it tomorrow:
If not, he must die of starvation and sorrow.

Says the Ant to the Cricket, 'I'm your servant and friend,
But we ants never borrow, we ants never lend;

But tell me, dear sir, did you lay nothing by
When the weather was warm?' Said the Cricket, 'Not I.
      My heart was so light
      That I sang day and night,
      For all nature looked gay.'
      'You *sang*, sir, you say?
Go then,' said the Ant, 'and *dance* winter away!'
    Thus ending, he hastily lifted the wicket
And out of the door turned the poor little Cricket.

Anon

THE SLUGGARD

'TIS the voice of the sluggard; I heard him complain—
'You have waked me too soon; I must slumber again.'
As the door on its hinges, so he on his bed,
Turns his sides, and his shoulders, and his heavy head.
'A little more sleep, and a little more slumber'—
Thus he wastes half his days, and his hours without number;
And when he gets up, he sits folding his hands,
Or walks about saunt'ring, or trifling he stands.

I passed by his garden, and saw the wild briar,
The thorn and the thistle grow broader and higher;
The clothes that hang on him are turning to rags;
And his money still wastes till he starves or he begs.
I made him a visit, still hoping to find
That he took better care for improving his mind;
He told me his dreams, talked of eating and drinking,
But he scarce reads his Bible, and never loves thinking.
Said I then to my heart: 'Here's a lesson for me;
That man's but a picture of what I might be;
But thanks to my friends for their care in my breeding,
Who taught me betimes to love working and reading.'

Isaac Watts

LITTLE THINGS

FOR want of a nail, the shoe is lost;
For want of a shoe, the horse is lost;
For want of a horse, the rider is lost;
For want of a rider, the battle is lost;
For want of a battle, the kingdom is lost;
And all for the want of a horseshoe nail.

Traditional

FESTINA LENTE

WHATEVER course of Life great Jove allots,
Whether you sit on thrones, or dwell in cots,
Observe your steps; be careful to command
Your passions; guide the reins with steady hand,
Nor down steep cliffs precipitately move
Urg'd headlong on by hatred or by love:
Let Reason with superior force control
The floods of rage, and calm thy ruffled soul.
Rashness! thou spring from whence misfortunes flow!
Parent of ills! and source of all our woe!
Thou to a scene of bloodshed turn'st the Ball,
By thee whole cities burn, whole nations fall!
By thee Orestes plung'd his vengeful dart
Into his supplicating mother's heart.
Hurried to death by thee, Flaminius fell,
And crowds of godlike Romans sunk to hell.
But cautious Fabius from impending fate
Preserv'd the relics of the Latian state
From bold invaders, clear'd th' Italian lands
And drove the swarthy troops to their own barren sands.

Samuel Johnson

PRAYER

GIVE me a good digestion, Lord,
And also something to digest;
Give me a healthy body, Lord,
   With sense to keep it at its best;
Give me a healthy mind, good Lord,
   To keep the good and pure in sight,

Which seeing sin is not appalled
    But finds a way to set it right;
Give me a mind that is not bored,
    That does not whimper, whine or sigh;
Don't let me worry overmuch
    About the fussy thing called I.
Give me a sense of humour, Lord,
    Give me the grace to see a joke,
To get some happiness from life
    And pass it on to other folk.

Found in Chester Cathedral

KING HENRY ON RESPONSIBILITY

UPON the King! Let us our lives, our souls,
Our debts, our careful wives,
Our children, and our sins lay on the King!
We must bear all. O hard condition,
Twin-born with greatness, subject to the breath
Of every fool, whose sense no more can feel
But his own wringing! What infinite heart's ease
Must kings neglect that private men enjoy!
And what have kings that privates have not too,
Save ceremony—save general ceremony?
And what art thou, thou idol Ceremony?
What kind of god art thou, that suffer'st more
Of mortal griefs than do thy worshippers?
What are thy rents? What are thy comings-in?
O Ceremony, show me but thy worth!
What is thy soul of adoration?
Art thou aught else but place, degree, and form,
Creating awe and fear in other men?
Wherein thou art less happy being fear'd
Than they in fearing.
What drink'st thou oft, instead of homage sweet,
But poison'd flattery? O, be sick, great greatness,
And bid thy ceremony give thee cure!
Thinks thou the fiery fever will go out
With titles blown from adulation?
Will it give place to flexure and low-bending?
Canst thou, when thou command'st the beggar's knee,

Command the health of it? No, thou proud dream,
That play'st so subtly with a king's repose.
I am a king that find thee; and I know
'Tis not the balm, the sceptre, and the ball,
The sword, the mace, the crown imperial,
The intertissued robe of gold and pearl,
The farced title running 'fore the king,
The throne he sits on, nor the tide of pomp
That beats upon the high shore of this world—
No, not all these, thrice-gorgeous ceremony,
Not all these, laid in bed majestical,
Can sleep so soundly as the wretched slave,
Who, with a body fill'd and vacant mind,
Gets him to rest, cramm'd with distressful bread;
Never sees horrid night, the child of hell;
But, like a lackey, from the rise to set
Sweats in the eye of Phœbus, and all night
Sleeps in Elysium; next day, after dawn,
Doth rise and help Hyperion to his horse;
And follows so the ever-running year
With profitable labour to his grave.
And, but for ceremony, such a wretch,
Winding up days with toil and nights with sleep,
Had the fore-hand and vantage of a king.
The slave, a member of the country's peace,
Enjoys it; but in gross brain little wots
What watch the king keeps to maintain the peace,
Whose hours the peasant best advantages.

William Shakespeare, from King Henry the Fifth

ON A QUIET CONSCIENCE

CLOSE thine eyes, and sleep secure;
Thy soul is safe, thy body sure.
He that guards thee, he that keeps,
Never slumbers, never sleeps.
A quiet conscience in the breast
Has only peace, has only rest.
The wisest and the mirth of kings
Are out of tune unless she sings:

Then close thine eyes in peace and sleep secure,
No sleep so sweet as thine, no rest so sure.

Charles Stuart, King Charles I

THE LADY POVERTY

THE Lady Poverty was fair:
But she has lost her looks of late,
With change of times and change of air.
Ah slattern! she neglects her hair,
Her gown, her shoes; she keeps no state
As once when her pure feet were bare.

Or—almost worse, if worse can be—
She scolds in parlours, dusts and trims,
Watches and counts. Oh, is this she
Whom Francis met, whose step was free,
Who with Obedience carolled hymns,
In Umbria walked with Chastity?

Where is her ladyhood? Not here,
Not among modern kinds of men;
But in the stony fields, where clear
Through the thin trees the skies appear,
In delicate spare soil and fen,
And slender landscape and austere.

Alice Meynell

TO BE A PILGRIM

WHO would true valour see,
Let him come hither!
One here will constant be
  Come wind, come weather;
There's no discouragement
Shall make him once relent
His first avowed intent
  To be a Pilgrim.

Whoso beset him round
  With dismal stories,

Do but themselves confound;
   His strength the more is.
No lion can him fright;
He'll with a giant fight;
But he will have the right
   To be a Pilgrim.

Hobgoblin, nor foul fiend
   Can daunt his spirit;
He knows he at the end
   Shall Life inherit.
Then fancies flee away;
He'll fear not what men say;
He'll labour night and day
   To be a Pilgrim.

John Bunyan

THE JOY OF SINS FORGIVEN

YE that do your Master's will,
   Meek in heart be meeker still:
Day by day your sins confess,
Ye that walk in righteousness:
Gracious souls in grace abound,
Seek the Lord, whom ye have found.

He that comforts all that mourn
Shall to joy your sorrow turn:
Joy to know your sins forgiven,
Joy to keep the way of heaven,
Joy to win His welcome grace,
Joy to see Him face to face.

Charles Wesley, from Short Hymns on Passages of the Holy Scriptures

THE UNIVERSAL PRAYER

FATHER of All! in every Age,
   In every Clime ador'd,
By Saint, by Savage, and by Sage,
   Jehovah, Jove, or Lord!

Thou Great First Cause, least Understood!
　　Who all my Sense confin'd
To know but this,—that Thou art Good,
　　And that my self am blind:

Yet gave me, in this dark Estate,
　　To see Good from Ill;
And binding Nature fast in Fate,
　　Left free the Human Will.

What Conscience dictates to be done,
　　Or warns me not to do,
This, teach me more than Hell to shun,
　　That, more than Heav'n pursue.

What Blessings Thy free Bounty gives,
　　Let me not cast away;
For God is pay'd when Man receives,
　　T' enjoy, is to obey.

Yet not to Earth's contracted Span,
　　Thy Goodness let me bound;
Or think Thee Lord alone of Man,
　　When thousand Worlds are round.

Let not this weak, unknowing hand
　　Presume Thy Bolts to throw,
And deal Damnation round the land,
　　On each I judge Thy Foe.

If I am right, oh teach my Heart
　　Still in the right to stay;
If I am wrong, Thy Grace impart
　　To find the better Way.

Save me alike from foolish Pride,
　　And impious Discontent,
At ought Thy Wisdom had deny'd,
　　Or ought Thy Goodness lent.

Teach me to feel another's Woe;
　　To hide the Fault I see;
That Mercy I to others show,
　　That Mercy show to me.

Mean tho' I am, not wholly so
   Since quicken'd by Thy Breath,
O lead me wheresoe'er I go,
   Thro' this day's Life, or Death:

This day, be Bread and Peace my Lot;
   All else beneath the Sun,
Thou know'st if best bestow'd, or not;
   And let Thy Will be done.

Alexander Pope, from a pendant to The Essay on Man

THE BEATITUDES

BLESSED are the poor in spirit:
   For their's is the kingdom of heaven.
Blessed are they that mourn:
   For they shall be comforted.
Blessed are the meek:
   For they shall inherit the earth.
Blessed are they which do hunger and thirst after righteousness:
   For they shall be filled.
Blessed are the merciful:
   For they shall obtain mercy.
Blessed are the pure in heart:
   For they shall see God.
Blessed are the peacemakers:
   For they shall be called the children of God.
Blessed are they which are persecuted for righteousness' sake:
   For their's is the kingdom of heaven.
Blessed are ye, when men shall revile you, and persecute you,
   And shall say all manner of evil against you falsely, for my sake.
Rejoice, and be exceeding glad:
  For great is your reward in heaven:
For so persecuted they the prophets which were before you.

St Matthew's Gospel, from The Holy Bible

LET US NOW PRAISE FAMOUS MEN

LET us now praise famous men,
And our fathers that begat us.
The Lord manifested in them great glory,
    Even his mighty power from the beginning.
Such as did bear rule in their kingdoms,
    And were men renowned for their power,
Giving counsel by their understanding,
    Such as have brought tidings in prophesies:
Leaders of the people by their counsels,
    And by their understanding
Men of learning for the people;
    Wise were their words in their instruction:
Such as sought out musical tunes,
    And set forth verses in writing:
Rich men furnished with ability,
    Living peaceably in their habitations:
All these were honoured in their generations,
    And were a glory in their days.
There be of them, that have left a name behind them,
    To declare their praises.
And some there be, which have no memorial;
    Who are perished as though they had not been,
And are become as though they had not been born;
    And their children after them.
But these were men of mercy,
    Whose righteous deeds have not been forgotten.
With their seed shall remain continually a good inheritance;
    Their children are in their testaments.
Their seed standeth fast,
    And their children for their sakes.
Their seed shall remain for ever,
    And their glory shall not be blotted out.
Their bodies were buried in peace,
    And their name liveth to all generations.
People will declare their wisdom,
    And the congregation telleth out their praise.

The Book of Ecclesiasticus, from The Apocrypha of The Holy Bible

SHE IS MY COUNTRY STILL

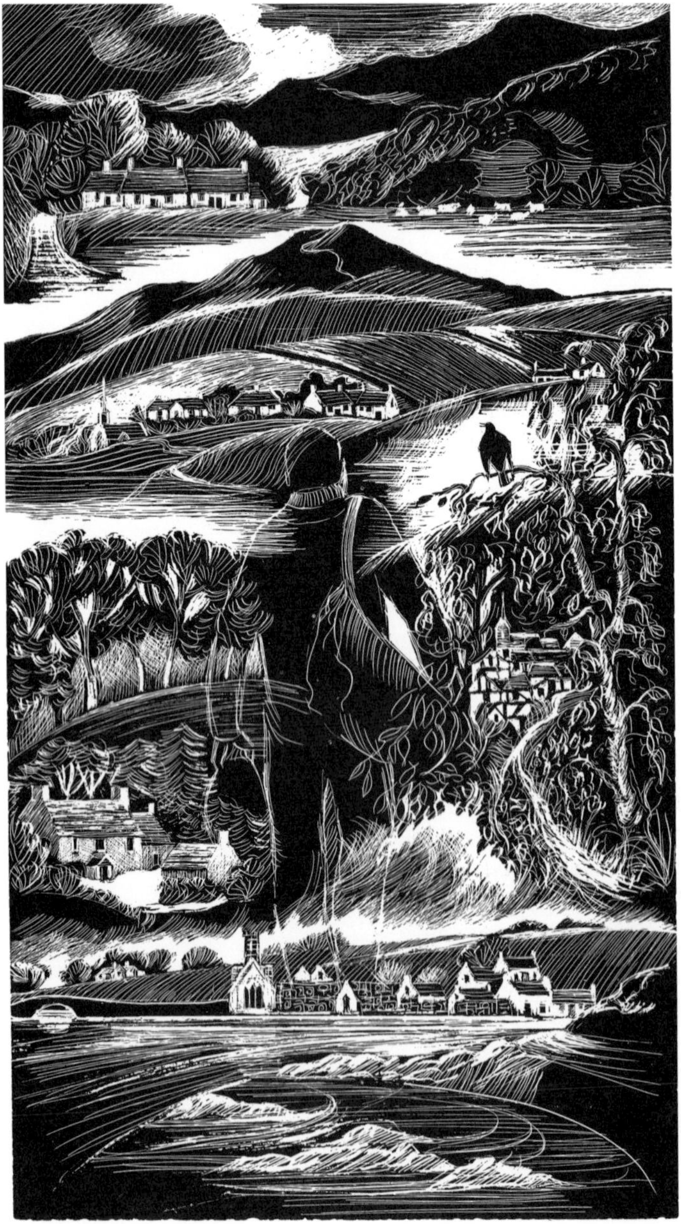

MY NATIVE LAND

BREATHES there the man, with soul so dead,
Who never to himself hath said,
　This is my own, my native land!
Whose heart hath ne'er within him burn'd,
As home his footsteps he hath turn'd,
　From wandering on a foreign strand!
If such there breathe, go, mark him well;
For him no Minstrel raptures swell;
High though his titles, proud his name,
Boundless his wealth as wish can claim;
Despite those titles, power, and pelf,
The wretch, concentrated all in self,
Living, shall forfeit fair renown,
And, doubly dying, shall go down
To the vile dust, from whence he sprung,
Unwept, unhonour'd, and unsung.

Sir Walter Scott, from The Lay of the Last Minstrel

THE ROAD TO THE ISLES

A FAR croonin' is pullin' me away
As take I wi' my cromak to the road.
The far Coolins are puttin' love on me
As step I wi' the sunlight for my load.

Sure, by Tummel and Loch Rannoch and Lochaber I will go,
By heather tracks wi' heaven in their wiles;
If it's thinkin' in your inner heart braggart's in my step,
You've never smelt the tangle o' the Isles.
Oh, the far Coolins are puttin' love on me,
As step I wi' my cromak to the Isles.

It's by Sheil water and the track is to the west,
By Aillort and by Morar to the sea,
The cool cresses I am thinkin' o' for pluck,
And bracken for a wink on Mother knee. *(chorus)*

It's the blue Islands are pullin' me away.
Their laughter puts the leap upon the lame,
The blue Islands from the Skerries to the Lews,
Wi' heather honey taste upon each name. *(chorus)*　　*Traditional*

SCOTLAND THE BRAVE

HARK! when the night is falling,
Hear! hear the pipes are calling,
Loudly and proudly calling,
   Down thro' the glen.
There where the hills are sleeping,
Now feel the blood a-leaping,
High as the spirits of the old Highland men.

> *Towering in gallant fame,*
> *Scotland my mountain hame,*
> *High may your proud standards gloriously wave,*
> *Land of my high endeavour,*
> *Land of the shining river,*
> *Land of my heart for ever,*
> *Scotland the brave!*

High in the misty Highlands,
Out by the purple islands,
Brave are the hearts that beat
   Beneath Scottish skies.
Wild are the winds to meet you,
Staunch are the friends that greet you,
Kind as the love that shines from fair maiden's eyes. *(chorus)*

Far off in sunlit places,
Sad are the Scottish faces,
Yearning to feel the kiss
   Of sweet Scottish rain,
Where tropic skies are beaming,
Love sets the heart a-dreaming,
Longing and dreaming for the homeland again. *(chorus)*

Traditional

EDINBURGH FROM THE PENTLAND HILLS

STILL on the spot Lord Marmion stay'd,
For fairer scene he ne'er survey'd.
   When sated with the martial show
   That peopled all the plain below,
   The wandering eye could o'er it go,
   And mark the distant city glow

    With gloomy splendour red;
For on the smoke-wreaths, huge and slow,
That round her sable turrets flow,
    The morning beams were shed,
And ting'd them with a lustre proud,
Like that which streaks a thunder-cloud.
Such dusky grandeur cloth'd the height,
Where the huge Castle holds its state,
    And all the steep slope down,
Whose ridgy back heaves to the sky,
Pil'd deep and massy, close and high,
    Mine own romantic town!
But northward far, with purer blaze,
On Ochil mountains fell the rays,
And as each heathy top they kiss'd,
It gleam'd a purple amethyst.
Yonder the shores of Fife you saw;
Here Preston-Bay and Berwick-Law:
    And, broad between them roll'd,
The gallant Frith the eye might note,
Whose islands on its bosom float,
    Like emeralds chas'd in gold.

Sir Walter Scott, from Marmion

THE SKYE BOAT SONG

SPEED bonnie boat like a bird on the wing,
Onward, the sailors cry.
Carry the lad that's born to be king
Over the sea to Skye.

Loud the winds howl, loud the waves roar,
Thunderclaps rend the air,
Baffled, our foes stand by the shore,
Follow they will not dare. *(chorus)*

Though the waves leap, soft shall ye sleep,
Ocean's a royal bed,
Rock'd in the deep, Flora will keep
Watch o'er your weary head. *(chorus)*

Burned are our homes, exile and death,
Scattered the loyal man,
Yet ere the sword, cool in the sheath,
Charlie will come again. *(chorus)*

Traditional

PONT-Y-WERN

DENBIGHSHIRE

WHEN soft September brings again
    To yonder gorse its golden glow,
And Snowdon sends its autumn rain
    To bid thy current livelier flow;
Amid the ashen foliage light
When scarlet beads are glistering bright,
While alder boughs unchanged are seen
In summer livery of green;
When clouds before the cooler breeze
Are flying, white and large; with these
Returning, so may I return
And find thee changeless, Pont-y-Wern.

Arthur Hugh Clough

THE ASH GROVE

LLWYN ON

THE ash grove how graceful, how plainly 'tis speaking,
    The harp thro' it playing has language for me;
Whenever the light thro' its branches is breaking,
    A host of kind faces is gazing on me.
The friends of my childhood again are before me,
    Each step wakes a memr'y as freely I roam,
With soft whispers laden, its leaves rustle o'er me,
    The ash grove, the ash grove alone is my home.

My lips smile no more, my heart loses its lightness,
    No dream of the future my spirit can cheer,
I only would brood on the past and its brightness,
    The dead I have mourned are again living here.
From ev'ry dark nook they press forward to meet me,
    I lift up my eyes to the broad leafy dome,

And others are there looking downward to greet me,
The ash grove, the ash grove alone is my home.

Welsh traditional, with English words by John Oxenford

THE HARP THAT ONCE THRO' TARA'S HALLS

THE harp that once thro' Tara's halls
The soul of music shed,
Now hangs as mute on Tara's walls
    As if that soul were fled.
So sleeps the pride of former days,
    So glory's thrill is o'er,
And hearts, that once beat high for praise,
    Now feel that pulse no more.

No more to chiefs and ladies bright
    The harp of Tara swells;
The cord alone, that breaks at night,
    Its tale of ruin tells.
Thus freedom now so seldom wakes,
    The only throb she gives
Is when some heart indignant breaks,
    To show that still she lives.

Thomas Moore

THE WEARIN' O' THE GREEN

OH,—Paddy dear! an' did ye hear the news that's goin' round?
The shamrock is forbid by law to grow on Irish ground!
Saint Patrick's day no more we'll kape, his colour can't be seen,
For there's a cruel law agin the wearin' o' the green!
I met wid Napper Tandy, and he tuk me by the hand,
And he said, 'How's poor ould Ireland, and how does she stand?'
'She's the most distressful counthery that iver yet was seen,
For they're hangin' men and women there: for wearin' o' the green!'

She's the most distressful counthery that iver yet was seen,
For they're hangin' men and women there: for wearin' o' the green!

Then since the colour we must wear is England's cruel red,
Sure Ireland's sons will ne'er forget the blood that they have shed;
You may pull the shamrock from your hat, and cast it on the sod,

But 'twill take root and flourish there, tho' underfoot 'tis trod!
When laws can stop the blades of grass from growin' as they grow,
And when the leaves in summertime their verdure dare not show,
Then I will change the colour too, I wear in my caubeen,
But till that day, plaze God! I'll stick to wearin' o' the green! *(chorus)*

But if at last our colour should be torn from Ireland's heart,
Her sons, with shame and sorrow, from the dear ould isle will part;
I've heard a whisper of a land that lies beyond the sea,
Where rich and poor stand equal in the light of freedom's day.
Ah! Erin! must we leave you, driven by a tyrant's hand?
Must we seek a mother's blessing from a strange and distant land?
Where the cruel cross of England shall never more be seen,
And where, plaze God, we'll live and die, still wearin' o' the green! *(chorus)*

Traditional

HEART OF OAK

COME, cheer up, my lads, 'tis to glory we steer,
To add something new to this wonderful year,
To honour we call you, not press you like slaves,
For who are so free as the sons of the waves?

>   *Heart of oak are our ships,*
>   *Jolly Tars are our men,*
>   *We always are ready:*
>   *Steady, boys, steady:*
>   *We'll fight and we'll conquer again and again.*

We ne'er see our foes but we wish them to stay;
They never see us, but they wish us away;
If they run, why, we follow, or run them ashore,
For if they won't fight us we cannot do more. *(chorus)*

They swear they'll invade us, these terrible foes!
They frighten our women, our children and beaux;
But should their flat bottoms in darkness get o'er,
Still Britons they'll find to receive them on shore. *(chorus)*

We'll still make them fear and we'll still make them flee,
And drub them on shore as we've drubbed them at sea;

Then cheer up, my lads, with one heart let us sing,
Our soldiers, our sailors, our statesmen, our King. *(chorus)*

David Garrick

RULE BRITANNIA

WHEN Britain first, at Heaven's command,
    Arose, from out the azure main,
This was the Charter, the Charter of the land,
    And guardian angels sang this strain—

Rule, Britannia, Britannia, rule the waves;
Britons never will be slaves.

The nations not so blest as thee
    Must, in their turn, to tyrants fall,
Whilst thou shalt flourish, great and free,
    The dread and envy of them all. *(chorus)*

Still more majestic shalt thou rise,
    More dreadful from each foreign stroke;
As the loud blast, that tears the skies,
    Serves but to root thy native oak. *(chorus)*

Thee, haughty tyrants ne'er shall tame;
    All their attempts to bend thee down
Will but arouse thy gen'rous flame,
    And work *their* woe, and *thy* renown.*(chorus)*

To thee belongs the rural reign,
    Thy cities shall with commerce shine;
All thine shall be the subject main,
    And ev'ry shore it circles, thine. *(chorus)*

The Muses, still with freedom found,
    Shall to thy happy coast repair;
Blest Isle! with matchless beauty crown'd,
    And manly hearts to guard the fair. *(chorus)*

James Thomson, from The Masque of Alfred

THIS SCEPT'RED ISLE

THIS royal throne of kings, this scept'red isle,
This earth of majesty, this seat of Mars,
This other Eden, demi-paradise,
This fortress built by Nature for herself
Against infection and the hand of war,
This happy breed of men, this little world,
This precious stone set in the silver sea,
Which serves it in the office of a wall,
Or as a moat defensive to a house,
Against the envy of less happier lands;
This blessed plot, this earth, this realm, this England,
This nurse, this teeming womb of royal kings,
Fear'd by their breed, and famous by their birth,
Renowned for their deeds as far from home,
For Christian service and true chivalry,
As is the sepulchre in stubborn Jewry
Of the world's ransom, blessed Mary's son;
This land of such dear souls, this dear dear land,
Dear for her reputation through the world,
Is now leas'd out—I die pronouncing it—
Like to a tenement or pelting farm.
England, bound in with the triumphant sea,
Whose rocky shore beats back the envious siege
Of wat'ry Neptune, is now bound in with shame,
With inky blots and rotten parchment bonds;
That England, that was wont to conquer others,
Hath made a shameful conquest of itself.
Ah, would the scandal vanish with my life,
How happy then were my ensuing death!

William Shakespeare, from King Richard the Second

JERUSALEM

AND did those feet in ancient time
Walk upon England's mountains green?
And was the holy Lamb of God
   On England's pleasant pastures seen?

And did the Countenance Divine
   Shine forth upon our clouded hills?

And was Jerusalem builded here
    Among these dark Satanic Mills?

Bring me my bow of burning gold!
    Bring me my arrows of desire!
Bring me my spear! O clouds, unfold!
    Bring me my chariot of fire!

I will not cease from mental fight,
    Nor shall my sword sleep in my hand,
Till we have built Jerusalem
    In England's green and pleasant land.

William Blake

HOME-THOUGHTS FROM ABROAD

OH to be in England
Now that April's there,
And whoever wakes in England
Sees, some morning, unaware,
That the lowest boughs and the brushwood sheaf
Round the elm-tree bole are in tiny leaf,
While the chaffinch sings on the orchard bough
In England—now!

And after April, when May follows,
And the whitethroat builds, and all the swallows!
Hark, where my blossomed pear-tree in the hedge
Leans to the field and scatters on the clover
Blossoms and dewdrops—at the bent spray's edge—
That's the wise thrush; he sings each song twice over,
Lest you should think he never would recapture
The first fine careless rapture!
And though the fields look rough with hoary dew,
All will be gay when noontide wakes anew
The buttercups, the little children's dower
—Far brighter than this gaudy melon-flower!

Robert Browning

COMPOSED UPON WESTMINSTER BRIDGE

SEPTEMBER 3rd, 1802

EARTH has not anything to show more fair:
Dull would he be of soul who could pass by
A sight so touching in its majesty:
The City now doth, like a garment, wear
The beauty of the morning; silent, bare,
Ships, towers, domes, theatres, and temples lie
Open unto the fields, and to the sky;
All bright and glittering in the smokeless air.
Never did sun more beautifully steep
In his first splendour, valley, rock, or hill;
Ne'er saw I, never felt, a calm so deep!
The river glideth at his own sweet will:
Dear God! the very houses seem asleep;
And all that mighty heart is lying still!

William Wordsworth

ENGLAND

ENGLAND with all thy faults, I love thee still—
My country! and, while yet a nook is left
Where English minds and manners may be found,
Shall be constrain'd to love thee. Though thy clime
Be fickle, and thy year must part deform'd
With dripping rains, or wither'd by a frost,
I would not yet exchange thy sullen skies,
And fields without a flow'r, for warmer France
With all her vines; nor for Ausonia's groves
Of golden fruitage, and her myrtle bow'rs.

William Cowper, from The Task

THE HEARTH OF HOME

THERE is a spot, 'mid barren hills,
   Where winter howls, and driving rain;
But if the dreary tempest chills,
   There is a light that warms again.

The house is old, the trees are bare,
   Moonless above bends twilight's dome;

But what on earth is half so dear—
    So longed for—as the hearth of home.

The mute bird sitting on the stone,
    The dank moss dripping from the wall,
The thorn-trees gaunt, the walks o'ergrown,
    I love them—how I love them all!...

A little and a lone green lane
    That opened on a common wide;
A distant, dreamy, dim blue chain
    Of mountains circling every side.

A heaven so clear, an earth so calm,
    So sweet, so soft, so hushed an air;
And, deepening still the dream-like charm,
Wild moor-sheep feeding everywhere....

Emily Brontë

GOD SAVE THE QUEEN

GOD save our gracious Queen,
Long live our noble Queen,
    God save the Queen!
Send her victorious,
Happy and glorious,
Long to reign over us;
    God save the Queen.

Thy choicest gifts in store,
On her be pleased to pour,
    Long may she reign;
May she defend our laws,
And ever give us cause
To say with heart and voice
    God save the Queen.

God bless our native land,
May heaven's protecting hand
    Still guard our shore;
May peace her power extend,
Foe be transformed to friend,

And Britain's rights depend
  On war no more.

May just and righteous laws
Uphold the public cause,
  And bless our isle.
Home of the brave and free,
The land of liberty,
We pray that still on thee
  Kind heaven may smile.

Nor on this land alone—
But be God's mercies known
  From shore to shore.
Lord, make the nations see
That men should brothers be,
And form one family
  The wide world o'er.

Traditional and W.E. Hickson

OVER THE HILLS AND FAR AWAY

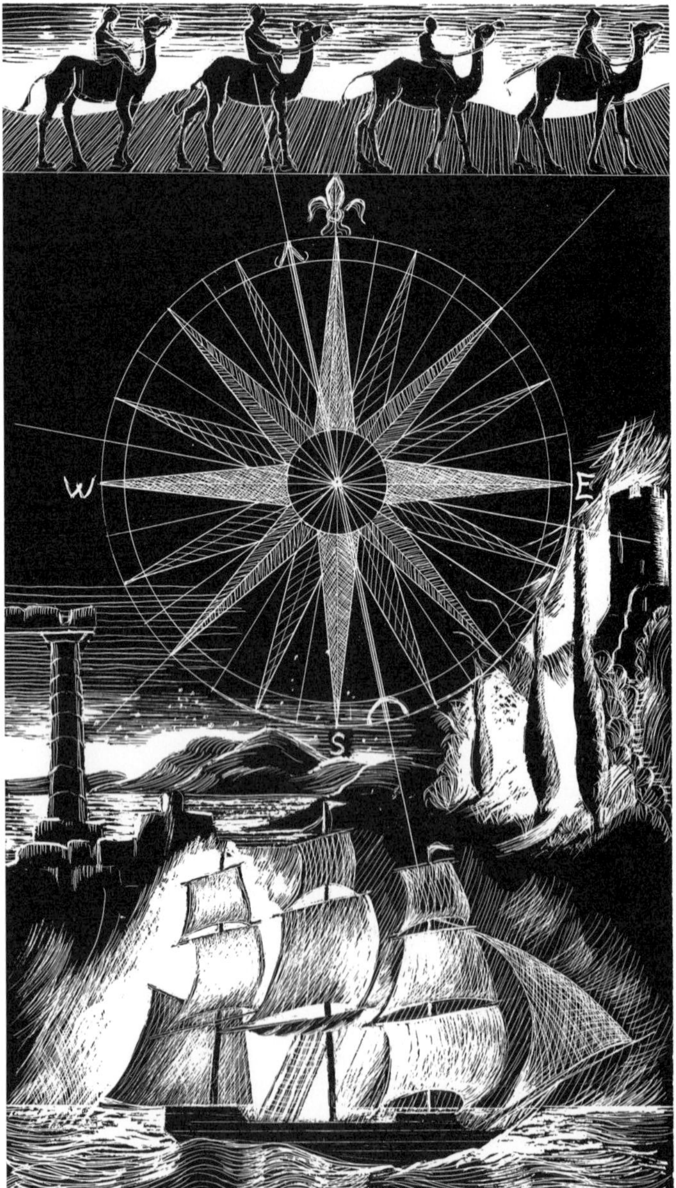
W
E
S

PILGRIMAGES TO CANTERBURY

WHAN that Aprille with his shoures sote
The droghte of Marche hath perced to the rote,
And bathed every veyne in swich licour
Of which vertu engendred is the flour;
Whan Zephirus eek with his swete breeth
Inspired hath in every holt and heeth
The tendre croppes, and the yonge sonne
Hath in the Ram his halfe cours y-ronne,
And smale fowles maken melodye,
That slepen al the night with open eye,—
(So priketh hem Nature in hir corages):—
Than longen folk to goon on pilgrimages
(And palmers for to seken straunge strondes)
To ferne halwes, cowthe in sondry londes;
And specially, from every shires ende
Of Engelond, to Caunterbury they wende,
The holy blisful martir for to seke,
That hem hath holpen, whan that they were seke.

Geoffrey Chaucer from The Prologue to the Canterbury Tales

FAREWELL TO OLD ENGLAND

FAREWELL to Old England for ever,
Farewell to our rum-culls as well;
Farewell to the well-loved Old Bailey
    Where I used for to cut such a swell

> *Singing too-ra-lie, too-ra-lie, addity,*
> *Singing too-ra-lie, too-ra-lie, aye,*
> *Singing too-ra-lie, too-ra-lie, addity,*
> *We're sailing for Botany Bay.*

'Taint leaving Old England we cares about,
    'Taint 'cause we mis-spells what we knows;
But because all we light-fingered gentry
    Hops around with a log on our toes. *(chorus)*

There's the captain as is our commandier,
    There's the bosun and all the ship's crew,
There's the first and the second class passengers
    Knows what we poor convicts goes through. *(chorus)*

For fourteen long years I'm transported,
    For fourteen long years and a day,
Just for meeting a cove in the alleyway,
    And stealing his ticker away. *(chorus)*

Oh, had I the wings of a turtle-dove!
    I'd soar on my pinions so high;
Slap bang to the arms of my Polly-love,
    And in her sweet bosom I'd die. *(chorus)*

Now, all you young dukies and duchesses,
    Take warning from what I do say,
Mind all is your own as you touchesses,
    Or you'll meet us in Botany Bay. *(chorus)*

Popular song based on a street ballad

VERSES OF ALEXANDER SELKIRK

Supposed to be written while he lived alone on the Island of Juan Fernandez

I AM monarch of all I survey,
    My right there is none to dispute;
From the centre all round to the sea,
    I am lord of the fowl and the brute.
O Solitude! where are the charms
    That sages have seen in thy face?
Better dwell in the midst of alarms
    Than reign in this horrible place.

I am out of humanity's reach,
    I must finish my journey alone,
Never hear the sweet music of speech,
    I start at the sound of my own.
The beasts that roam over the plain
    My form with indifference see;
They are so unacquainted with man,
    Their tameness is shocking to me.

Society, friendship and love,
    Divinely bestowed upon man,
O, had I the wings of a dove,
    How soon would I taste you again!
My sorrows I then might assuage,

OVER THE HILLS AND FAR AWAY

In the ways of religion and truth,
Might learn from the wisdom of age,
    And be cheer'd by the sallies of youth.

Religion! what treasure untold
    Lies hid in that heavenly word!
More precious than silver or gold,
    Or all that this earth can afford.
But the sound of the church-going bell,
    These valleys and rocks never heard,
Never sigh'd at the sound of the knell,
    Or smiled when a sabbath appear'd.

Ye winds that have made me your sport,
    Convey to this desolate shore
Some cordial, endearing report
    Of a land I shall visit no more.
My friends, do they now and then send
    A wish or a thought after me?
O, tell me I yet have a friend,
    Though a friend I am never to see.

How fleet is a glance of the mind!
    Compar'd with the speed of its flight,
The tempest himself lags behind
    And the swift-winged arrows of light.
When I think of my own native land,
    In a moment I seem to be there;
But, alas! recollection at hand
    Soon hurtles me back to despair.

But the sea-fowl is gone to her nest,
    The beast is laid down in his lair;
Even here is a season of rest,
    And I to my cabin repair.
There's mercy in every place,
    And mercy, encouraging thought,
Gives even affliction a grace,
    And reconciles man to his lot.

William Cowper

THE OLD SHIPS

I HAVE seen old ships sail like swans asleep
Beyond the village which men still call Tyre,
With leaden age o'ercargoed, dipping deep
For Famagusta and the hidden sun
That rings black Cyprus with a lake of fire;
And all those ships were certainly so old
Who knows how oft with squat and noisy gun,
Questing brown slaves or Syrian oranges,
The pirates Genoese
Half-raked them till they rolled
Blood, water, fruit and corpses up the hold.
But now through friendly seas they softly run,
Painted the mid-sea blue or shore-sea green,
Still patterned with the vine and grapes in gold.

But I have seen,
Pointing her shapely shadows from the dawn
And image tumbled on a rose-swept bay,
A drowsy ship of some yet older day;
And, wonder's breath indrawn,
Thought I—who knows—who knows— but in that same
(Fished up beyond Ææa, patched up new
—Stern painted brighter blue—)
That talkative, bald-headed seaman came
(Twelve patient comrades sweating at the oar)
From Troy's doom-crimson shore,
And with great lies about his wooden horse
Set the crew laughing, and forgot his course.

It was so old a ship—who knows, who knows?
—And yet so beautiful, I watched in vain
To see the mast burst open with a rose,
And the whole deck put on its leaves again.

James Elroy Flecker

OZYMANDIAS

I MET a traveller from an antique land
Who said: 'Two vast and trunkless legs of stone
Stand in the desert…Near them, on the sand,
Half sunk, a shattered visage lies, whose frown,
And wrinkled lip, and sneer of cold command,
Tell that its sculptor well those passions read
Which yet survive, stamped on these lifeless things,
The hand that mocked them, and the heart that fed:
And on the pedestal these words appear:
"My name is Ozymandias, king of kings:
Look on my works, ye Mighty, and despair!"
Nothing beside remains. Round the decay
Of that colossal wreck, boundless and bare
The lone and level sands stretch far away.'

Percy Bysshe Shelley

THE ISLES OF GREECE

THE isles of Greece, the isles of Greece!
   Where burning Sapho loved and sung,
Where grew the arts of war and peace,
   Where Delos rose, and Phœbus sprung!
Eternal summer gilds them yet,
But all, except their sun, is set.

The Scian and the Telian muse,
   The hero's harp, the lover's lute,
Have found the fame your shores refuse:
   Their place of birth alone is mute
To sounds which echo further west
Than your sires' 'Islands of the Blest.'

The mountains look on Marathon—
   And Marathon looks on the sea;
And musing there an hour alone,
   I dream'd that Greece might still be free;
For standing on the Persians' grave,
I could not deem myself a slave.

A king sate on the rocky brow
   Which looks o'er sea-born Salamis;

And ships, by thousands, lay below,
    And men in nations ;—all were his!
He counted them at break of day—
    And when the sun set where were they?

And where are they? and where art thou,
    My country? On thy voiceless shore
The heroic lay is tuneless now—
    The heroic bosom beats no more!
And must thy lyre, so long divine,
Degenerate into hands like mine?

'Tis something, in the dearth of fame,
    Though link'd among a fetter'd race,
To feel at least a patriot's shame,
    Even as I sing, suffuse my face;
For what is left the poet here?
For Greeks a blush—for Greece a tear.

Must *we* but weep o'er days more blest?
    Must *we* but blush?—Our fathers bled.
Earth! render back from out thy breast
    A remnant of our Spartan dead!
Of the three hundred grant but three,
To make a new Thermopylæ!

What, silent still? and silent all?
    Ah! no; —the voices of the dead
Sound like a distant torrent's fall,
    And answer, 'Let one living head,
But one arise,—we come, we come!'
'Tis but the living who are dumb.

In vain—in vain: strike other cords;
    Fill high the cup with Samian wine!
Leave battles to the Turkish hordes.
    And shed the blood of Scio's vine!
Hark! rising to the ignoble call—
How answers each bold Bacchanal!

You have the Pyrrhic dance as yet;
    Where is the Pyrrhic phalanx gone?
Of two such lessons, why forget

The nobler and the manlier one?
You have the letters Cadmus gave—
Think ye he meant them for a slave?

Fill high the bowl with Samian wine!
    We will not think of themes like these!
It made Anacreon's song divine:
    He served—but served Polycrates—
A tyrant; but our master then
Were still, at least, our countrymen.

The tyrant of the Chersonese
    Was freedom's best and bravest friend;
That tyrant was Miltiades!
    Oh! that the present hour would lend
Another despot of the kind!
Such chains as his were sure to bind.

Fill high the bowl with Samian wine!
    On Suli's rock, and Parga's shore,
Exists the remnant of a line
    Such as the Doric mothers bore;
And there, perhaps, some seed is sown,
The Heracleidan blood might own.

Trust not for freedom to the Franks—
    They have a king who buys and sells;
In native swords, and native ranks,
    The only hope of courage dwells:
But Turkish force, and Latin fraud,
Would break your shield, however broad.

Fill high the bowl with Samian wine!
    Our virgins dance beneath the shade—
I see their glorious black eyes shine;
    But gazing on each glowing maid,
My own the burning tear-drop laves,
To think such breasts must suckles slaves.

Place me on Sunium's marbled steep,
    Where nothing, save the waves and I,
May hear our mutual murmurs sweep;
    There, swan-like, let me sing and die:

A land of slaves shall ne'er be mine—
Dash down yon cup of Samian wine!

George Gordon, Lord Byron

'DE GUSTIBUS—'

I

YOUR ghost will walk, you lover of trees,
    (If our loves remain)
    In an English lane,
By a cornfield-side a-flutter with poppies.
Hark, those two in the hazel coppice—
A boy and a girl, if the good fates please,
    Making love, say—
    The happier they!
Draw yourself up from the light of the moon,
And let them pass, as they will too soon,
    With the bean-flowers' boon,
    And the blackbird's tune,
    And May, and June!

II

What I love best in all the world
Is a castle, precipice-encurled,
In a gash of wind-grieved Apennine.
Or look for me, old fellow of mine,
(If I get my head from out the mouth
O' the grave, and loose my spirit's bands,
And come again to the land of lands)—
In a sea-side house to the farther South,
Where the baked cicala dies of drouth,
And one sharp tree—'tis a cypress—stands,
By the many hundred years red-rusted,
Rough iron-spiked, ripe fruit-o'ercrusted,
My sentinel to guard the sands
To the water's edge. For, what expands
Before the house, but the great opaque
Blue-breadth of sea without a break?
While, in the house, for ever crumbles
Some fragment of the frescoed walls,
From blisters where a scorpion sprawls.

A girl bare-footed brings, and tumbles
Down on the pavement, green-flesh melons,
And says there's news to-day—the king
Was shot at, touched in the liver-wing,
Goes with his Bourbon arm in a sling:
—She hopes they have not caught the felons.
Italy, my Italy!
Queen Mary's saying serves for me—
      (When fortune's malice
        Lost her—Calais)—
Open my heart and you will see
Graved inside of it, 'Italy.'
Such lovers old are I and she:
So it always was, so shall ever be!

Robert Browning

FLORENCE

I FOUND a house at Florence on the hill
Of Bellosguardo. 'Tis a tower which keeps
A post of double-observation o'er
That valley of Arno (holding as a hand
The outspread city,) straight toward Fiesole
And Mount Morello and the setting sun,
The Vallombrosan mountains opposite,
Which sunrise fills as full as crystal cups
Turned red to the brim because their wine is red.
No sun could die nor yet be born unseen
By dwellers at my villa: morn and even
Were magnified before us in the pure
Illimitable space and pause of sky,
Intense as angels' garments blanched with God,
Less blue than radiant. From the outer wall
Of the garden, drops the mystic floating gray
Of olive -trees, (with interruptions green
From maize and vine) until 'tis caught and torn
Upon the abrupt black line of cypresses
Which signs the way to Florence. Beautiful
The city lies along the ample vale,
Cathedral, tower and palace, piazza and street,
The river trailing like a silver cord

Through all, and curling loosely, both before
And after, over the whole stretch of land
Sown whitely up and down its opposite slopes
With farms and villas.

Elizabeth Barrett Browning

THE GOLDEN JOURNEY TO SAMARKAND

At the Gate of the Sun, Bagdad, in olden time

THE MERCHANTS

AWAY, for we are ready to a man!
Our camels sniff the evening and are glad.
Lead on, O Master of the Caravan:
 Lead on the Merchant-Princes of Bagdad.

THE CHIEF DRAPER

Have we not Indian carpets dark as wine,
 Turbans and sashes, gowns and bows and veils,
And broideries of intricate design,
 And printed hangings in enormous bales?

THE CHIEF GROCER

We have rose-candy, we have spikenard,
 Mastic and terebinth and oil and spice,
And such sweet jams meticulously jarred
 As God's own prophet eats in Paradise.

THE PRINCIPAL JEWS

And we have manuscripts in peacock styles
 By Ali of Damascus; we have swords
Engraved with storks and apes and crocodiles,
 And heavy beaten necklaces, for Lords.

THE MASTER OF THE CARAVAN

But you are nothing but a lot of Jews.

THE PRINCIPAL JEWS

Sir, even dogs have daylight, and we pay.

OVER THE HILLS AND FAR AWAY

MASTER OF THE CARAVAN

But who are ye in rags and rotten shoes,
    You dirty-bearded, blocking up the way?

THE PILGRIMS

We are the Pilgrims, master; we shall go
    Always a little farther; it may be
Beyond that last blue mountain barred with snow,
    Across that angry or that glimmering sea,

White on a throne or guarded in a cave
    There lives a prophet who can understand
Why men were born: but surely we are brave,
    Who make the Golden Journey to Samarkand.

THE CHIEF MERCHANT

We gnaw the nail of hurry. Master, away!

ONE OF THE WOMEN

    O turn your eyes to where your children stand.
Is not Bagdad the beautiful? O stay!

THE MERCHANTS *(IN CHORUS)*

We take the Golden Road to Samarkand.

AN OLD MAN

Have you not girls and garlands in your homes,
    Eunuchs and Syrian boys at your command?
Seek not excess: God hateth him who roams!

THE MERCHANTS *(IN CHORUS)*

We make the Golden Journey to Samarkand.

A PILGRIM WITH A BEAUTIFUL VOICE

Sweet to ride forth at evening from the wells
    When shadows pass gigantic on the sand,
And softly through the silence beat the bells
    Along the Golden Road to Samarkand.

A MERCHANT

We travel not for trafficking alone:
  By hotter winds our fiery hearts are fanned:
For lust of knowing what should not be known
  We make the Golden Jounrey to Samarkand.

THE MASTER OF THE CARAVAN

Open the gate, O watchman of the night!

THE WATCHMAN

Ho, travellers, I open. For what land
Leave you the dim-moon city of delight?

THE MERCHANTS

(with a shout)

We make the Golden Journey to Samarkand.

(The caravan passes through the gate)

THE WATCHMAN

(consoling the women)

What would ye, ladies? It was ever thus,
  Men are unwise and curiously planned.

A WOMAN

They have their dreams, and do not think of us.

VOICE OF THE CARAVAN

(in the distance, singing)

We make the Golden Journey to Samarkand

James Elroy Flecker, from Hassan

I WHISTLE AND I SING

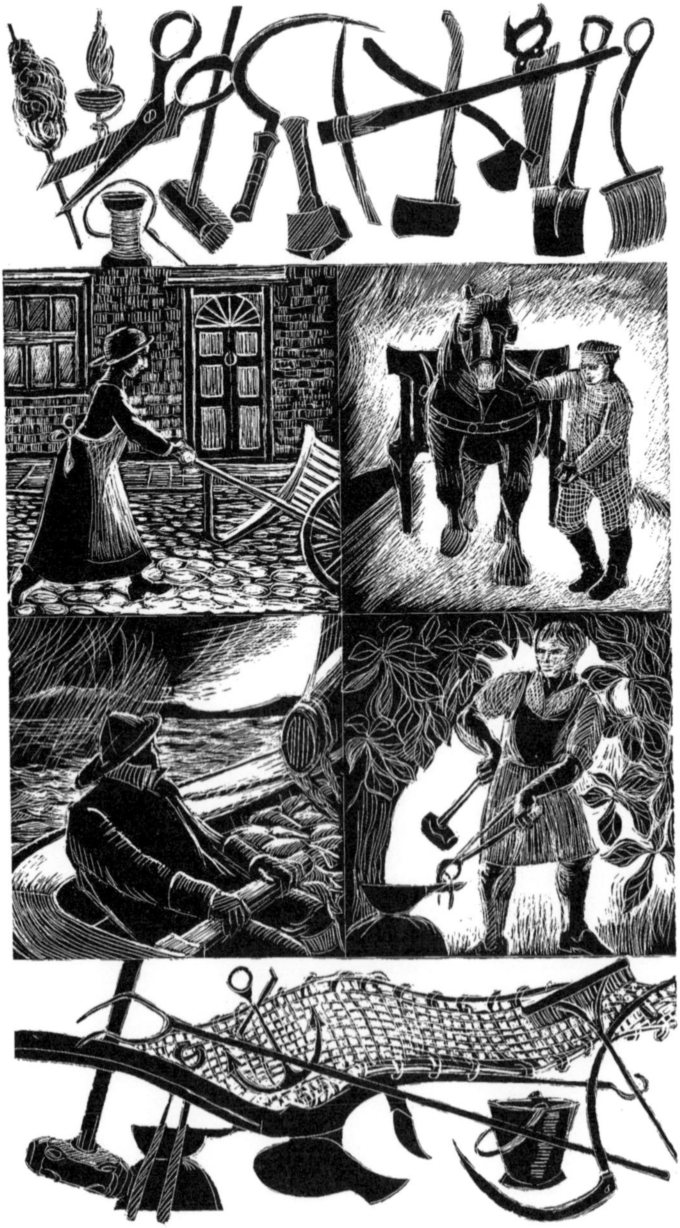

JIM THE CARTER LAD

ME name is Jim, the carter lad,
A jolly cock am I!
I always am contented
Be the weather wet or dry.
I crack me fingers at the snow
And whistle in the rain,
And I've braved the storm for many a day,
And can do so again.

> *So it's crack, crack, goes me whip,*
> *I whistle and I sing.*
> *I sit upon me wagon,*
> *I'm as happy as a king.*
> *Me horse is always willing,*
> *And for me, I'm never sad:*
> *There's none can lead a jollier life*
> *Nor Jim, the carter lad.*

Me father was a carrier,
Many years e'er I was born;
He used to rise at daybreak
And go his round each morn.
He would often take me with him,
Especially in the spring,
When I loved to sit upon the cart,
And hear me father sing. *(chorus)*

It's now the girls all smile on me,
As I go driving past:
The horse is such a beauty,
As we jog along so fast.
We've travell'd many weary miles,
But happy days we've had;
And there's none can use a horse more kind
Nor Jim, the carter lad. *(chorus)*

Now, friends, I bid you all: Adieu.
'Tis time I was away.
I know me horse will weary
If I much longer stay.
To see your smiling faces here,

It makes me feel quite glad,
And I'll know you'll grant your kind applause
To Jim, the carter lad. *(chorus)*

Traditional

THE QUEEN OF CONNEMARA

O MY boat can sweetly float
In the teeth of wind and weather,
And outsail the fastest hooker
'Tween Galway and Kinsale.
When the wide rim of the ocean
And the wild waves rush together,
O she rides in her pride
Like a seabird in the gale.

> *O she's neat, O she's sweet!*
> *She's a beauty ev'ry line!*
> *The Queen of Connemara*
> *Is the bounding barque o' mine!*

When she's loaded down with fish
Till the water laves the gunwale,
Not a drop she'll take aboard her
That will wash a fly away.
From the beach she speeds out quickly
Like a greyhound from her kennel,
Till she lands her silv'ry store,
The first on old Kinvarra quay. *(chorus)*

There's a light that shines afar,
And it keeps me from dismaying,
When the clouds are ink above us,
And the sea runs white with foam.
In a cot in Connemara,
There's a wife and wee one praying
To the One who walked the waters once,
To guide us safely home. *(chorus)*

Irish Traditional

COCKLES AND MUSSELS

IN Dublin's fair city,
Where girls are so pretty,
I first set my eyes on sweet Molly Malone,
As she wheeled her wheel barrow
Through streets broad and narrow,
Crying, 'Cockles and Mussels!
Alive, alive oh!'

> *'Alive, alive oh! Alive, alive oh!'*
> *Crying, 'Cockles and mussels!*
> *Alive, alive oh!'*

She was a fishmonger
But sure 'twas no wonder,
For so were her father and mother before,
And they each wheeled their barrow
Through streets broad and narrow,
Crying, 'Cockles and mussels!
Alive, alive oh!' *(chorus)*

She died of a fever,
And no one could save her,
And that was the end of sweet Molly Malone;
But her ghost wheels her barrow,
Through streets broad and narrow,
Crying, 'Cockles and mussels!
Alive, alive oh!' *(chorus)*

Irish Traditional

JOHN BARLEYCORN

THERE was three Kings into the East,
   Three Kings both great and high,
And they hae sworn a solemn oath
   John Barleycorn should die

They took a plough and plough'd him down,
   Put clods upon his head,
And they hae sworn a solemn oath
   John Barleycorn was dead.

But the cheerf'l Spring came kindly on,
    And show'rs began to fall;
John Barleycorn got up again,
    And sore surpris'd them all.

The sultry suns of Summer came,
    And he grew thick and strong,
His head well arm'd wi' pointed spears,
    That no one should him wrong.

The sober Autumn enter'd mild,
    When he grew wan and pale;
His bending joints and drooping head
    Shew'd he began to fail.

His colour sicken'd more and more,
    He faded into age;
And then his enemies began
    To shew their deadly rage.

They've ta'en a weapon, long and sharp,
    And cut him by the knee;
And tied him fast upon a cart,
    Like a rogue for forgerie.

They laid him down upon his back,
    And cudgell'd him full sore;
They hung him up before the storm,
    And turn'd him o'er and o'er.

They fillèd up a darksome pit
    With water to the brim,
They heavèd in John Barleycorn,
    There let him sink or swim.

They laid him out upon the floor,
    To work him farther woe,
And still, as signs of life appear'd,
    They toss'd him to and fro.

They wasted, o'er a scorching flame,
    The marrow of his bones;
But a miller used him worst of all,
    For he crush'd him between two stones.

And they hae ta'en his very heart's blood,
    And drank it round and round;
And still the more and more they drink,
    Their joy did more abound.

John Barleycorn was a hero bold,
    Of noble enterprise;
For if you do but taste his blood,
    'Twill make your courage rise.

'Twill make a man forget his woe;
    'Twill heighten all his joy:
'Twill make the widow's heart to sing,
    Tho' the tears were in her eye.

Then let us toast John Barleycorn,
    Each man a glass in hand;
And may his great posterity
    Ne'er fail in old Scotland!

Robert Burns, version of an Old Ballad

THE HOCK-CART

HARVEST HOME

COME, sons of summer, by whose toil
We are the lords of wine and oil;
By whose tough labours and rough hands
We rip up first, then reap our lands,
Crowned with the ears of corn, now come,
And, to the pipe, sing 'Harvest-home.'
Come forth, my Lord, and see the cart
Dressed up with all the country art.
See, here a maukin, there a sheet,
As spotless pure as it is sweet;
The horses, mares, and frisking fillies,
Clad all in linen, white as lilies.
The harvest swains and wenches bound
For joy to see the Hock-Cart crowned.
About the cart hear how the rout
Of rural younglings raise the shout;
Pressing before, some coming after,
Those with a shout, and these with laughter.

Some bless the cart, some kiss the sheaves,
Some prank them up with oaken leaves;
Some cross the fill-horse, some with great
Devotion stroke the home-borne wheat;
While other rustics, less attent
To prayers than to merriment,
Run after with their breeches rent.
Well, on, brave boys, to your Lord's hearth,
Glitt'ring with fire; where, for your mirth,
Foundation of your feast—fat beef,
With upper storeys, mutton, veal
And bacon, (which makes the full meal)
With sev'ral dishes standing by,
As here a custard, there a pie,
And here all-tempting frumenty.
And for to make the merry cheer,
If smirking wine be wanting here,
There's that, which drowns all care—stout beer;
Which freely drink to your Lord's health,
Then to the plough, the Common-wealth,
Next to your flails, your vanes, your vats;
Then to the maids with wheaten hats;
To the rough sickle and crooked scythe;
Drink, frolic, boys, till all be blithe.
Feed, and grow fat, and as you eat,
Be mindful, that the labouring neat
(As you) may have their fill of meat.
And know, besides, you must revoke
The patient ox unto the yoke,
And all go back unto the plough
And harrow, (though they're hanged up now.)
And, you must know, your Lord's word's true,
Feed him ye must, whose food fills you.
And that this pleasure is like rain,
Not sent for you to drown your pain,
But for to make it spring again.

Robert Herrick

THE PRETTY PLOUGHBOY

AS I was a-walking
  One morning in Spring,
I heard a pretty ploughboy,
  And so sweetly he did sing:
And as he was a-singing O
  These words I heard him say:
'There's no life like the ploughboy's
  In the sweet month of May.

There's the lark in the morning
  She will rise up from her nest,
And she'll mount the white air
  With the dew on her breast,
She's whistle and she'll sain
  And at night she'll return
To her nest back again.'

Traditional

SIX JOLLY MINERS

HERE come six jolly miners,
  We're not worth a pin,
But when we get a bit of coal
  We'll make the kettle sing!

> *So we'll riddle and we'll fiddle*
> *And we'll make the earth go round.*
> *If you don't mind your troubles*
> *You will have a motty-down*[1].

Two came from Derby,
  And two from Derby town,
The others came from Oughterbridge,
  And they all came firing down. *(chorus)*

We've travelled all of England,
  Scotland and Ireland round
And all of our delight
  Is in working underground. *(chorus)*

All our delight, boys,
  Is to split the rocks in time;

Our pleasure it is more than that
  In working underground. *(chorus)*

We'll call for liquors plenty,
  And let the drinks go round;
Here's health to the jolly miner lad
  That works down underground! *(chorus)*

Sometimes we have money,
  But now we've none at all,
And since you have good credit
  It's upon you we do call. *(chorus)*

Traditional

1. Motty down: a miners' token, exchangeable for coal.,accepted as payment for goods in mining areas..

THE VILLAGE BLACKSMITH

UNDER a spreading chestnut-tree
  The village smithy stands;
The smith, a mighty man is he,
  With large and sinewy hands;
And the muscles of his brawny arms
  Are strong as iron bands.

His hair is crisp, and black, and long,
  His face is like the tan;
His brow is wet with honest sweat,
  He earns whate'er he can,
And looks the whole world in the face,
  For he owes not any man.

Week in, week out, from morn till night,
  You can hear his bellows blow,
You can hear him swing his heavy sledge,
  With measured beat and slow,
Like a sexton ringing the village bell,
  When the evening sun is low.

And children coming home from school
  Look in at the open door;
They love to see the flaming forge,
  And hear the bellows roar,
And catch the burning sparks that fly
  Like chaff from a threshing floor.

He goes on Sunday to the church,
    And sits among his boys;
He hears the parson pray and preach,
    He hears his daughter's voice
Singing in the village choir,
    And it makes his heart rejoice:—

It sounds to him like her mother's voice,
    Singing in Paradise!
He needs must think of her once more,
    How in the grave she lies;
And with his hard, rough hand he wipes
    A tear out of his eyes.

Toiling, —rejoicing,—sorrowing,
    Onward through life he goes;
Each morning sees some task begin,
    Every evening sees its close;
Something attempted, something done,
    Has earned a night's repose.

Thanks, thanks to thee, my worthy friend
    For the lesson thou hast taught!
Thus at the flaming forge of life
    Our fortunes must be wrought;
Thus on its sounding anvil shaped
    Each burning deed and thought!

Henry Longfellow

THE FRUIT OF HER HANDS

WHO can find a virtuous woman?
    For her price is far above rubies.
The heart of her husband doth safely trust in her,
    So that he shall have no need of spoil.
She will do him good and not evil
    All the days of her life.
She seeketh wool, and flax,
    And worketh willingly with her hands.
She is like the merchants' ships;
    She bringeth her food from afar.
She riseth also when it is yet night,

And giveth meat to her household,
And a portion to her maidens.

She considereth a field, and buyeth it:
    With the fruit of her hands she planteth a vineyard.
She girdeth her loins with strength,
    And strengtheneth her arms.
She perceiveth that her merchandise is good:
    Her candle goeth not out by night.
She layeth her hands to the spindle,
    And her hands hold the distaff.

She stretcheth out her hand to the poor;
    Yea, she reacheth forth her hands to the needy.
She is not afraid of the snow for her household:
    For all her household are clothed with scarlet.
She maketh herself coverings of tapestry;
    Her clothing is silk and purple.
Her husband is known in the gates,
    When he sitteth among the elders of the land.
She maketh fine linen, and selleth it;
    And delivereth girdles unto the merchant.

Strength and honour are her clothing;
    And she shall rejoice in time to come.
She openeth her mouth with wisdom;
    And in her tongue is the law of kindness.
She looketh well to the ways of her household,
    And eateth not the bread of idleness.
Her children arise up, and call her blessed;
    Her husband also, and he praiseth her.

Many daughters have done virtuously,
    But thou excellest them all.
Favour is deceitful,
    And beauty is vain:
But a woman that feareth the Lord,
    She shall be praised.
Give her of the fruit of her hands;
    And let her own works praise her in the gates.

Book of Proverbs from The Holy Bible

THE ELIXIR

TEACH me my God and King,
  In all things thee to see;
And what I do in anything
  To do it as for Thee!

Not rudely, as a beast,
  To run into an action;
But still to make Thee prepossest
  And give it his perfection.

A man that looks on glass,
  On it may stay his eye;
Or if he pleaseth, through it pass,
  And then the heav'n espy.

All may of Thee partake:
  Nothing can be so mean,
Which with his tincture, 'for Thy sake,'
  Will not grow bright and clean.

A servant with this clause
  Makes drudgery divine;
Who sweeps a room, as for Thy laws,
  Makes that and th' action fine.

This is the famous stone
  That turneth all to gold:
For that which God doth touch and own
  Cannot for less be told.

George Herbert

THE SONG OF THE GUARDIAN ANGEL

MY work is done,
My task is o'er,
And so I come,
Taking it home.
For the crown is won,
Alleluia,
For evermore.

My father gave
In charge to me
This child of earth
E'en from its birth,
To serve and save,
Alleluia,
And saved is he.

This child of clay
To me was given,
To rear and train
By sorrow and pain
In the narrow way,
Alleluia,
From earth to heaven.

John Henry, Cardinal Newman, from the Dream of Gerontius

BEHOLD,
I SHEW YOU A MYSTERY

PATER
NON EST
FILIUS
EST
EST
DEUS
NON EST
NON EST
EST
SPIRITUS SANCTUS

THE SPACIOUS FIRMAMENT ON HIGH

THE spacious firmament on high,
With all the blue ethereal sky,
And spangled heavens, a shining frame,
Their great Original proclaim.
Th' unwearied Sun from day to day
Does his Creator's power display;
And publishes to every land
The work of an Almighty hand.

Soon as the evening shades prevail,
The Moon takes up the wondrous tale;
And nightly to the listening Earth
Repeats the story of her birth:
Whilst all the stars that round her burn,
And all the planets in their turn,
Confirm the tidings as they roll,
And spread the truth from pole to pole.

What though in solemn silence all
Move round the dark terrestrial ball;
What though nor real voice nor sound
Amidst their radiant orbs be found?
In Reason's ear they all rejoice,
And utter forth a glorious voice;
For ever singing as they shine,
'The Hand that made us is divine.'

Joseph Addison

ALL THINGS BRIGHT AND BEAUTIFUL

ALL things bright and beautiful,
All creatures great and small,
All things wise and wonderful,
    The Lord God made them all.

Each little flower that opens,
    Each little bird that sings,
He made their glowing colours,
    He made their tiny wings: *(refrain)*

The rich man in his castle,
  The poor man at his gate,
God made them high or lowly,
  And ordered their estate: *(refrain)*

The purple-headed mountains,
  The river running by,
The sunset and the morning,
  That brightens up the sky: *(refrain)*

The cold wind in the winter,
  The pleasant summer sun,
The ripe fruits in the garden—
  He made them every one: *(refrain)*

The tall trees in the greenwood,
  The meadows where we play,
The rushes by the water
  We gather every day: *(refrain)*.

He gave us eyes to see them,
  And lips that we might tell,
How great is God Almighty,
  Who has made all things well: *(refrain)*

Cecil Frances Alexander

THE FAITH OF JOB

FOR I know
That my redeemer liveth,
And that he shall stand
At the latter day upon the earth:
And though after my skin
Worms destroy this body,
Yet in my flesh
Shall I see God:
Whom I shall see for myself,
And mine eyes shall behold,
And not another;
Though my reins be consumed within me.

Book of Job, from The Holy Bible

THE PEOPLE THAT WALKED IN DARKNESS

THE people that walked in darkness
    Have seen a great light:
They that dwell in the land of the shadow of death,
    Upon them hath the light shined.
Thou hast multiplied the nation,
    And not increased the joy:
They joy before thee according to the joy in harvest,
    And as men rejoice when they divide the spoil.
For thou hast broken the yoke of his burden,
    And the staff of his shoulder,
The rod of his oppressor,
    As in the days of Midian.
For every battle of the warrior is with confused noise,
    And garments rolled in blood;
But this shall be with burning and fuel of fire.

For unto us a child is born,
    Unto us a son is given:
And the government shall be upon his shoulder:
    And his name shall be called Wonderful, Counsellor,
The mighty God, the everlasting Father,
    The Prince of Peace.

Of the increase of his government and peace
    There shall be no end, upon the throne of David,
And upon his kingdom, to order it,
    And to establish it with judgment and justice
From henceforth even for ever.

The zeal of the Lord of hosts will perform this.

Book of Isaiah, from The Holy Bible

THE LORD IS MY SHEPHERD

THE Lord is my shepherd;
    I shall not want.
He maketh me to lie down in green pastures:
    He leadeth me beside still waters.

    He restoreth my soul:
He leadeth me in the paths of righteousness

For his name's sake.
Yea, though I walk through the valley of the shadow of death,
    I will fear no evil: for thou art with me;
Thy rod and thy staff they comfort me.

Thou preparest a table before me
    In the presence of mine enemies:
Thou anointest my head with oil:
    My cup runneth over.
Surely goodness and mercy shall follow me
    All the days of my life:
And I will dwell in the house of the Lord for ever.

The Twenty-third Psalm, from The Holy Bible

ADAM

ADAM lay y-bounden
    Bounden in a bond;
Four thousand winters
    Thought he not too long.

And all was for an apple,
    An apple that he took,
As clerkès finden written
    In their Book.

Ne had the apple taken been,
    The apple taken been,
Ne had never Our Lady
    A-been Heaven's Queen.

Blessèd be the time
    That apple taken was!
Therefore we moun singen
    Deo gratias!

Mediæval Carol

THE SEVEN VIRGINS

All under the leaves and the leaves of life
    I met with virgins seven,
And one of them was Mary mild
    Our Lord's mother of Heaven.

'Oh, what are you seeking, you seven fair maids
    All under the leaves of life?
Come tell, come tell, what seek you
    All under the leaves of life?'

'We're seeking for no leaves, Thomas,
    But for a friend of thine;
We're seeking for sweet Jesus Christ,
    To be our guide and thine.'

'Go down, go down, to yonder town,
    And sit in the gallery,
And there you'll see sweet Jesus Christ
    Nail'd to a big yew-tree.'

So down they went to yonder town,
    As fast as foot could fall,
And many a grievous bitter tear
    From the virgins' eyes did fall.

'O peace, Mother, O peace, Mother,
    Your weeping doth me grieve:
I must suffer this,' He said,
    'For Adam and for Eve.'

'O how can I my weeping leave,
    Or my sorrows undergo,
Whilst I do see my own son die
    When sons I have no mo'?'

'O Mother, take you John Evangelist
    All for to be your son,
And he will comfort you sometimes,
    Mother, as I have done.'

'O come, thou John Evangelist,
    Thou'rt welcome unto me,

But more welcome my own dear Son,
  Whom I nursèd upon my knee.'

Then He laid His head on His right shoulder,
  Seeing death it struck him nigh—
'The Holy Ghost be with your soul,
  I die, Mother dear, I die.'

O the rose, the rose, the gentle rose,
  And the fennel that grows so green!
God gave us grace in every place
  To pray for our king and queen.

Furthermore for our enemies all
  Our prayers they should be strong.
Amen, Good Lord! your charity
  Is the ending of my song.

Traditional

CALVARY

THERE is a green hill far away
  Without a city wall,
Where the dear Lord was crucified
  Who died to save us all.

We may not know, we cannot tell,
  What pains He had to bear,
But we do know it was for us
  He hung and suffered there.

He died that we might be forgiven,
  He died to make us good;
That we may go at last to Heaven,
  Saved by His Precious Blood.

There was no other good enough
  To pay the price of sin;
He only could unlock the gate
  Of heaven, and let us in.

O, dearly, dearly has He loved,
  And we must love Him too,

With all our strength and all our mind,
    And prove our love is true.

Cecil Frances Alexander

ST PATRICK'S BREASTPLATE

I

I BIND unto myself today
The strong name of the Trinity,
By invocation of the same,
    The Three in One, and One in Three.

I bind unto myself today
    The virtues of the star-lit heaven,
The glorious sun's life-giving ray,
    The whiteness of the moon at even,

The flashing of the lightning free,
    The whirling wind's tempestuous shocks,
The stable earth, the deep salt sea,
    Around the old eternal rocks.

I bind unto myself today
    The power of God to hold and lead,
His eye to watch, his might to stay,
    His ear to harken to my need;

The wisdom of my God to teach,
    His hand to guide, His shield to ward;
The word of God to give me speech,
    His heavenly host to be my guard.

II

Christ be with me, Christ within me,
    Christ behind me, Christ before me,
Christ beside me, Christ to win me,
    Christ to comfort and restore me,

Christ beneath me, Christ above me,
    Christ in quiet, Christ in danger,
Christ in hearts of all that love me,
    Christ in mouth of friend and stranger.

III

 I bind unto myself the name
  The strong name of the Trinity,
 By invocation of the same,
  The Three in One, and One in Three,

 Of whom all nature hath creation;
  Eternal Father, Spirit, Word:
 Praise to the Lord of my salvation:
  Salvation is of Christ the Lord.

Cecil Frances Alexander, based on a hymn of St Patrick

WE PRAISE THEE, O GOD

TE DEUM LAUDAMUS

WE praise Thee, O God: we acknowledge Thee to be the Lord.
All the earth doth worship Thee: the Father everlasting.
To Thee all angels cry aloud: the heavens and all the powers therein.
To Thee Cherubim and Seraphim: continually do cry,
Holy, Holy, Holy, Lord God of Sabaoth.
Heaven and earth are full of the Majesty of Thy glory.

The glorious company of the Apostles praise Thee.
The goodly fellowship of the Prophets praise Thee.
The noble army of Martyrs praise Thee.
The Holy Church throughout all the world doth acknowledge Thee;
The Father of an infinite Majesty;
Thine honourable, true, and only Son;
Also the Holy Ghost, the Comforter.

Thou art the King of Glory, O Christ.
Thou art the everlasting Son of the Father.
When Thou tookest upon Thee to deliver man,
Thou didst not abhor the Virgin's womb.
When Thou hadst overcome the sharpness of death,
Thou didst open the kingdom of heaven to all believers.
Thou sittest at the right hand of God, in the glory of the Father.

We believe that Thou shalt come to be our Judge.
We therefore pray Thee help Thy servants,
Whom Thou hast redeemed with Thy precious blood.
Make them to be numbered with Thy Saints in glory everlasting.

O Lord, save Thy people; and bless Thine inheritance.
Govern them; and lift them up for ever.

Day by day, we magnify Thee;
And we worship Thy name, ever world without end.
Vouchsafe, O Lord, to keep us this day without sin.
O Lord, have mercy upon us, have mercy upon us.
O Lord, let Thy mercy lighten upon us, as our trust is in Thee.
O Lord, in Thee have I trusted; let me never be confounded.

Traditional Hymn

PRAISE TO THE HOLIEST

PRAISE to the Holiest in the height,
    And in the depth be praise:
In all His words most wonderful;
    Most sure in all His Ways!

O loving wisdom of our God!
    When all was sin and shame,
A second Adam to the fight
    And to the rescue came.

O wisest love! that flesh and blood
    Which did in Adam fail,
Should strive afresh against the foe,
    Should strive and should prevail;

And that a higher gift than grace
    Should flesh and blood refine,
God's Presence and His very Self,
    And Essence all-divine.

O generous love! that He who smote
    In man for man the foe,
The double agony in man
    For man should undergo.

And in the garden secretly,
    And on the cross on high,
Should teach His brethren and inspire
    To suffer and to die.

John Henry, Cardinal Newman, from The Dream of Gerontius

GUIDE ME, O THOU GREAT REDEEMER

ARGLWYDD ARWAIN TRWY'R ANIALWCH

GUIDE me, O Thou great Redeemer,
Pilgrim through this barren land;
I am weak, but Thou art mighty,
   Hold me with Thy powerful hand:
      Bread of heaven,
Feed me till I want no more.

Open now the crystal fountain,
   Whence the healing stream doth flow;
Let the fire and cloudy pillar
   Lead me all my journey through:
      Strong Deliverer,
Be Thou still my strength and shield.

When I tread the verge of Jordan,
   Bid my anxious fears subside;
Death of death, and hell's Destruction,
   Land me safe on Canaan's side:
      Songs of praises
I will ever give to Thee.

Peter and William Williams

PRAYER

PRAYER the Church's banquet, Angels' age,
   God's breath in man returning to his birth,
   The soul in paraphrase, heart in pilgrimage,
The Christian plummet sounding heav'n and earth;
Engine against th'Almighty, sinners' tower,
   Reversed thunder, Christ-side-piercing spear,
   The six-days world transposing in an hour,
A kind of tune which all things hear and fear;
Softness, and peace and joy, and love, and bliss,
   Exalted Manna, gladness of the best,
   Heaven in ordinary, man well-dressed,
The milky way, the bird of Paradise,
   Church-bells beyond the stars heard, the soul's blood,
   The land of spices; something understood.

George Herbert

THE PILLAR OF THE CLOUD

LEAD, Kindly Light, amid the encircling gloom,
    Lead Thou me on!
The night is dark, and I am far from home—
    Lead Thou me on!
Keep Thou my feet; I do not ask to see
The distant scene—one step enough for me.

I was not ever thus, nor pray'd that Thou
    Shouldst lead me on.
I loved to choose and see my path, but now
    Lead Thou me on!
I loved the garish day, and, spite of fears,
Pride ruled my will: remember not past years.

So long Thy power hath blest me, sure it still
    Will lead me on,
O'er moor and fen, o'er crag and torrent, till
    The night is gone;
And with the morn those angel faces smile
Which I have loved long since, and lost awhile.

John Henry, Cardinal Newman

E TENEBRIS

COME down, O Christ, and help me! reach Thy hand,
  For I am drowning in a stormier sea
  Than Simon on thy lake of Galilee:
The wine of life is spilt upon the sand,
My heart is as some famine-murdered land
  Whence all good things have perished utterly,
  And well I know my soul in Hell must lie
If I this night before God's throne should stand.
  'He sleeps perchance, or rideth to the chase,
  Like Baal, when his prophets howled that name
  From morn to noon on Carmel's smitten height.'
Nay, peace, I shall behold, before the night,
  The feet of brass, the robe more white than flame,
The wounded hands, the weary human face.

Oscar Wilde

LOVE UNKNOWN

MY song is love unknown,
My Saviour's love to me,
Love to the loveless shown,
That they might lovely be.
O who am I,
That for my sake
My Lord should take
Frail flesh, and die?

He came from his blest throne,
Salvation to bestow;
But men made strange, and none
The longed-for Christ would know.
But O, my friend,
My friend indeed,
Who at my need
His life did spend!

Sometimes they strew His way,
And His sweet praises sing;
Resounding all the day
Hosannas to their king.
Then 'Crucify!'
Is all their breath,
And for His death
They thirst and cry.

Why, what hath my Lord done?
What makes this rage and spite?
He made the lame to run,
He gave the blind their sight.
Sweet injuries!
Yet they at these
Themselves displease,
And 'gainst Him rise.

They rise, and needs will have
My dear Lord made away;
A murderer they save,
The Prince of Life they slay.
Yet cheerful He

> To suffering goes,
> That He His foes
> From thence might free.

In life, no house, no home
  My Lord on earth might have:
In death, no friendly tomb
  But what a stranger gave.
    What may I say?
      Heaven was His home;
    But mine the tomb
  Wherein He lay.

Here might I stay and sing,
  No story so divine;
Never was love, dear King,
  Never was grief like Thine.
    This is my Friend,
      In whose sweet praise
    I all my days
  Could gladly spend.

Samuel Crossman

LOVE

LOVE bade me welcome: yet my soul drew back,
    Guilty of dust and sin.
But quick-eyed Love, observing me grow slack
    From my first entrance in,
Drew nearer to me, sweetly questioning,
    If I lack'd any thing.

'A guest,' I answer'd, 'worthy to be here:'
    Love said, 'You shall be he.'
'I the unkind, ungrateful? Ah my dear,
    I cannot look on thee.'
Love took my hand, and smiling did reply,
    'Who made the eyes but I?'

'Truth Lord, but I have marr'd them: let my shame
    Go where it doth deserve.'
'And know you not,' says Love, 'who bore the blame?'
    'My dear, then I will serve.'

'You must sit down,' says Love, 'and taste my meat:'
So I did sit and eat.

George Herbert

OF THE BLESSED SACRAMENT OF THE ALTAR

THE angels' eyes, whom veils cannot deceive,
   Might best disclose that best they do discern;
Men must with sound and silent faith receive
   More than they can by sense or reason learn;
God's power our proofs, His works our wit exceed,
The doer's might is reason of His deed.

A body is endued with ghostly rights;
   And Nature's work from Nature's law is free;
In heavenly sun lie hid eternal lights,
   Lights clear and near, yet them no eye can see;
Dead forms a never-dying life do shroud;
A boundless sea lies in a little cloud.

The God of Hosts in slender host doth dwell,
   Yea, God and man with all to either due,
That God that rules the heavens and rifled hell,
   That man whose death did us to life renew:
That God and man that is the angels' bliss,
In form of bread and wine our nurture is.

Whole may His body be in smallest bread,
   Whole in the whole, yea whole in every crumb;
With which be one or be ten thousand fed,
   All to each one, to all but one doth come;
And though each one as much as all receive,
Not one too much, nor all too little have.

One soul in man is all in every part;
   One face at once in many mirrors shines;
One fearful noise doth make a thousand start;
   One eye at once of countless things defines;
If proofs of one in many, Nature frame,
God may in stranger sort perform the same.

God present is at once in every place,
   Yet God in every place is ever one;

So may there be by gifts of ghostly grace,
   One man in many rooms, yet filling none;
Since angels may effects of bodies shew,
God angels' gifts on bodies may bestow.

Robert Southwell, Saint and Martyr

BREAD OF HEAVEN

O BREAD of Heaven, beneath this veil
  Thou dost my very God conceal:
My Jesus, dearest treasure, hail!
   I love Thee and adoring kneel;
Each loving soul by Thee is fed
With Thine Own Self in form of bread.

O Food of life, Thou who dost give
   The pledge of immortality;
I live; no, 'tis not I that live;
   God gives me life, God lives in me:
He feeds my soul, He guides my ways,
And every grief with joy repays.

O bond of love, that dost unite
   The servant to his living Lord;
Could I dare live, and not requite
   Such love—then death were meet reward:
I cannot live unless to prove
Some love for such unmeasured love.

Beloved Lord in Heaven above,
   There, Jesus, Thou awaitest me;
To gaze on Thee with changeless love;
   Yes, thus, I hope, thus shall it be:
For how can He deny me heaven
Who here on earth Himself hath given?

Edward Vaughan, based on a hymn of St Alphonsus Liguori

SOUL OF MY SAVIOUR

ANIMA CHRISTI

SOUL of my Saviour, sanctify my breast;
Body of Christ, be Thou my saving guest.
Blood of my Saviour, bathe me in Thy tide,
Wash me, ye Waters, flowing from Thy side!

Strength and protection may Thy Passion be;
O blessèd Jesu, hear and answer me;
Deep in Thy wounds, Lord, hide and shelter me,
So shall I never, never part from Thee.

Guard and defend me from the foe malign;
In death's dread moments make me only Thine.
Call me, and bid me come to Thee on high,
When I may praise Thee with Thy Saints for aye.

Traditional, and J Hegarty, from a Mediæval Latin Hymn

CROWN HIM WITH MANY CROWNS

CROWN Him with many crowns,
  The Lamb upon His throne;
Hark how the heavenly anthem drowns
  All music but its own:
  Awake, my soul, and sing
  Of Him who died for thee,
And hail Him as thy matchless King
  Through all eternity.

  Crown Him the Virgin's Son,
  The God Incarnate born,—
Whose arm those crimson trophies won
  Which now His Brow adorn!
  Fruit of the mystic Rose,
  As of that Rose the Stem;
The Root, whence Mercy ever flows,
  The Babe of Bethlehem.

  Crown Him the Lord of peace:
  Whose power a sceptre sways
From pole to pole, that wars may cease
  Absorbed in prayer and praise:

His reign shall know no end,
　　And round his piercèd feet
Fair flowers of Paradise extend
　　Their fragrance ever sweet.

Crown Him the Lord of heaven,
　　One with the Father known,
And the blest Spirit through Him given
　　From yonder triune throne:
　　All hail, Redeemer, hail,
　　For Thou hast died for me:
Thy praise shall never, never fail
　　Throughout eternity.

Crown Him the Lord of years,
　　The Potentate of time,
Creator of the rolling spheres,
　　Ineffably sublime:
　　Glazed in a sea of light,
　　Whose everlasting waves
Reflect His form, the Infinite,
　　Who lives and loves, and saves.

Matthew Bridges

O SAVING VICTIM

O SAVING Victim, opening wide
　　The gate of heav'n to Man below;
Our foes press on from every side;
　　Thine aid supply, thy strength bestow.

To Thy great name be endless praise,
　　Immortal Godhead, One in Three;
O grant us endless length of days
　　In our true native land with Thee.

Therefore we, before Him bending,
　　This great Sacrament revere;
Types and shadows have their ending,
　　For the newer rite is here;
Faith, our outward sense befriending,
　　Makes the inward vision clear.

Glory let us give, and blessing
    To the Father and the Son,
Honour, might and praise addressing,
    While eternal ages run;
Ever too His love confessing,
Who from both, with both is one.

Edward Caswall, J. M. Neale and others, after St. Thomas Aquinas

THE CONCEPTION OF OUR LADY

OUR second Eve puts on her mortal shroud,
    Earth breeds a heaven for God's new dwelling-place;
Now riseth up Elias' little cloud,
    That growing shall distil the shower of grace;
Her being now begins, who, ere she end
Shall bring the good that shall our evil amend.

Both Grace and Nature did their force unite
    To make this babe the sum of all their best;
Our most, her least, our million, but her mite,
    She was at easiest rate worth all the rest:
What Grace to men or angels God did part,
Was all united in this infant's heart.

Four only wights bred without fault are named,
    And all the rest conceivèd were in sin;
Without both man and wife was Adam framed,
    Of man, but not of wife, did Eve begin;
Wife without touch of man Christ's mother was,
Of man and wife this babe was bred in Grace.

Robert Southwell, Saint and Martyr

OUR LADY'S SONG

MAGNIFICAT

MY soul doth magnify the Lord,
    And my spirit hath rejoiced in God my Saviour.
For He hath regarded
    The low estate of His hand-maiden.
For, behold, from henceforth
    All generations shall call me blessed.
For he that is mighty hath done to me great things;

And holy is His name.
And His mercy is on them that fear him
   From generation to generation.

He hath shewed strength with His arm;
He hath scattered the proud
   In the imagination of their hearts.
He hath put down the mighty from their seats,
   And hath exalted them of low degree.
He hath filled the hungry with good things
   And the rich He hath sent empty away.
He hath holpen His servant Israel,
   In remembrance of His mercy;
As He spake to our fathers,
   To Abraham, and to his seed for ever.

St Luke's Gospel, from The Holy Bible

ON THE GLORIOUS ASSUMPTION OF OUR BLESSED LADY

HARK! she is call'd, the parting hour is come;
Take thy farewell, poor World! Heaven must go home.
A piece of heavenly light, purer and brighter
Than the chaste stars, whose choice lamps come to light her,
While through the crystal orbs, clearer than they,
She climbs, and makes a far more milky way.
She's call'd. Hark! how the dear immortal dove
Sighs to his silver mate, 'Rise up, my love!
Rise up, my fair, my spotless one!
The Winter's past, the rain is gone:
The Spring is come, the flowers appear,
No sweets, but thou, are wanting here.'

> *'Come away, my love!*
> *Come away, my dove,*
>   *Cast off delay;*
> *The court of Heav'n is come,*
> *To wait upon thee home;*
>   *Come away, come away.*

'The flowers appear,
Or quickly would, wert thou once here.
The Spring is come, or if it stay

'Tis to keep time with thy delay.
The rain is gone, except as much as we
Detain in needful tears to weep the want of thee.
    The Winter's past,
      Or if he make less haste
His answer is why she does so,
If Summer come not, how can Winter go?
    Come away, come away!
The shrill winds chide, the waters weep thy stay;
The fountains murmur, and each loftiest tree
Bows lowest his leafy top to look for thee.' *(refrain)*.

She's call'd again. And will she go?
When Heaven bids come, who can say no?
Heaven calls her, and she must away,
Heaven will not, and she cannot stay.
Go then; go, glorious on the golden wings
Of the bright youth of Heaven, that sings
Under so sweet a burthen. Go,
Since thy dread Son will have it so:
And while thou go'st, our song and we
Will, as we may, reach after thee.
Hail, holy queen of humble hearts!
We in thy praise will have our parts.

    Thy precious name shall be
    Thy self to us: and we
      With holy care will keep it by us,
        We to the last
        Will keep it fast,
      And no Assumption shall deny us.
    All the sweetest showers
    Of our fairest flowers
    Will we strew upon it.
    Though our sweets cannot make
    It sweeter, they can take
    Themselves new sweetness from it.

Maria, men and angels sing,
Maria, mother of our King.
Live, rosy princess, live! and may the bright
Crown of a most incomparable light

Embrace thy radiant brows! O may the best
Of everlasting joys bathe thy white breast.
Live, our chaste love, the holy mirth
Of Heaven; the humble pride of Earth.
Live, crown of women, queen of men.
Live, mistress of our song. And when
Our weak desires have done their best,
Sweet angels come, and sing the rest.

Richard Crashaw

HAIL, QUEEN OF HEAVEN

HAIL, Queen of Heaven, the ocean Star!
Guide of the wanderer here below:
Thrown on life's surge, we claim thy care,
    Save us from peril and from woe.
        Mother of Christ, Star of the sea,
        Pray for the wanderer, pray for me.

O gentle, chaste, and spotless Maid,
    We sinners make our prayers through thee;
Remind thy Son that he has paid
    The price of our iniquity.
        Virgin most pure, Star of the sea,
        Pray for the sinner, pray for me.

Sojourners in this vale of tears,
    To thee, blest advocate, we cry;
Pity our sorrows, calm our fears,
    And soothe with hope our misery.
        Refuge in grief, Star of the sea,
        Pray for the mourner, pray for me.

And while to Him who reigns above,
    In Godhead One, in Persons Three,
The Source of life, of grace, of love,
    Homage we pay on bended knee,
        Do thou, bright Queen, Star of the sea,
        Pray for thy children, pray for me.

John Lingard

BRING FLOWERS OF THE RAREST

BRING flowers of the rarest,
Bring blossoms the fairest,
From garden and woodland
  And hillside and dale;
Our full hearts are swelling,
Our glad voices telling
The praise of the loveliest
  Flower of the vale.

O Mary we crown thee with blossoms today.
Queen of the Angels and Queen of the May. (repeat)

Their Lady they name thee,
Their Mistress proclaim thee.
Oh grant that thy children
  On earth be as true;
As long as the bowers
Are radiant with flowers,
As long as the azure shall
  Keep its bright hue. *(chorus)*

Sing gaily in chorus:
The bright angels o'er us
Re-echo the strain we
  Begin upon earth;
Their harps are repeating
The notes of our greeting,
For Mary herself is the
  Cause of our mirth. *(chorus)*

Traditional hymn to Our Lady

THE KINGDOM OF GOD

O WORLD invisible, we view thee,
O world intangible, we touch thee,
O world unknowable, we know thee,
Inapprehensible, we clutch thee!

Does the fish soar to find the ocean,
The eagle plunge to find the air—

That we ask of the stars in motion
If they have rumour of thee there?

Not where the wheeling systems darken,
And our benumbed conceiving soars!—
The drift of pinions, would we harken,
Beats at our own clay-shuttered doors.

The angels keep their ancient places;—
Turn but a stone, and start a wing!
'Tis ye, 'tis your estrangèd faces,
That miss the many-splendoured thing.

But (when so sad thou canst not sadder)
Cry;—and upon thy so sore loss
Shall shine the traffic of Jacob's ladder
Pitched betwixt Heaven and Charing Cross.

Yea, in the night, my Soul, my daughter,
Cry,—clinging Heaven by the hems;
And lo, Christ walking on the water
Not of Gennesareth but Thames!

Francis Thompson

FAITH

FIRMLY I believe and truly
   God is Three, and God is One;
And I next acknowledge duly
   Manhood taken by the Son.
And I trust and hope most fully
   In that manhood crucified;
And each thought and deed unruly
   Do to death, as He has died.
Simply to His grace and wholly
   Light and life and strength belong,
And I love, supremely, solely,
   Him the holy, Him the strong.

And I hold in veneration,
   For the love of Him alone,
Holy Church, as His creation,
   And her teachings, as His own.

And I take with joy whatever
    Now besets me, pain or fear,
And with a strong will I sever
    All the ties which bind me here.
Adoration aye be given,
    With and through the angelic host,
To the God of earth and heaven,
    Father, Son, and Holy Ghost.

John Henry, Cardinal Newman, from the Dream of Gerontius

O GOD OUR HELP IN AGES PAST

O GOD our help in ages past,
    Our hope for years to come,
Our shelter from the stormy blast,
    And our eternal home;

Under the shadow of Thy throne
    Thy Saints have dwelt secure;
Sufficient is Thine arm alone,
    And our defence is sure.

Before the hills in order stood,
    Or earth received her frame,
From everlasting Thou art God,
    To endless years the same.

A thousand ages in Thy sight
    Are like an evening gone,
Short as the watch that ends the night
    Before the rising sun.

Time, like an ever-rolling stream,
    Bears all its sons away;
They fly forgotten, as a dream
    Dies at the opening day.

O God, our help in ages past,
    Our hope in years to come,
Be Thou our guard while troubles last,
    And our eternal home.

Isaac Watts

SIMEON'S SONG

NUNC DIMITTIS

LORD, now lettest Thou Thy servant depart in peace:
According to Thy word.
For mine eyes have seen
   Thy salvation;
Which Thou hast prepared
   Before the face of all people;
A light to lighten the Gentiles:
   And the glory of Thy people Israel.

St. Luke's Gospel, from The Holy Bible

FOR THE DYING OR DEPARTED

PROFISCERE ANIMA CHRISTIANA

GO forth upon thy journey, Christian soul!
Go from this world!
Go, in the name of God, the Omnipotent Father, who created thee.
Go, in the name of Jesus Christ, our Lord,
Son of the living God, who bled for thee.
Go, in the name of the Holy Spirit, who hath been pour'd out on thee!
Go, in the name of Mary, God's Holy and Glorious Virgin Mother;
In the name of her Great Consort, Blessed Joseph.

Go, in the name of Angels and Archangels,
Of Thrones and Dominations, of Principalities and Powers,
Of Virtues, Cherubim and Seraphim.
Go, in the name of Patriarchs and Prophets,
Of the Holy Apostles and Evangelists,
Of the Holy Martyrs and Confessors, of the Holy Monks and Hermits,
Of the Holy Virgins, and of all the Saints of God!
In peace be thy home this day and Holy Sion thine abode.

Traditional Prayer

IN THE HANDS OF GOD

BUT the souls of the righteous are in the hands of God,
And no torment shall touch them.
In the eyes of the foolish they seemed to have died;
   And their departure was accounted to be their hurt,

And their journeying away from us their ruin:
  But they are in peace.

For even if in the sight of men they be punished,
  Their hope is full of immortality;
And having borne a little chastening,
  They shall receive great good;
Because God made trial of them,
  And found them worthy of Himself.
As gold in the furnace he proved them,
  And as a whole burnt offering he accepted them.
And in the time of their visitation they shall shine forth,
  And as sparks among stubble they shall run to and fro.

They shall judge nations, and have dominion over peoples;
  And the Lord shall reign over them for evermore.
They that trust on him shall understand truth,
  And the faithful shall abide with him in love;
Because grace and mercy are to his chosen.

The Wisdom of Solomon, from The Holy Bible

FOR ALL THE SAINTS

FOR all the Saints who from their labours rest,
Who Thee by faith before the world confest,
Thy name, O Jesu, be for ever blest. *Alleluya!*

Thou wast their Rock, their Fortress, and their Might;
Thou, Lord, their Captain in the well-fought fight;
Thou in the darkness drear their one true Light. *Alleluya!*

O may Thy soldiers, faithful, true, and bold,
Fight as the Saints who nobly fought of old,
And win, with them, the victor's crown of gold. *Alleluya!*

O blest communion! fellowship divine!
We feebly struggle, they in glory shine;
Yet all are one in Thee, for all are Thine. *Alleluya!*

And when the strife is fierce, the warfare long,
Steals on the ear the distant triumph-song,
And hearts are brave again, and arms are strong. *Alleluya!*

The golden evening brightens in the west;
Soon, soon to faithful warriors cometh rest:
Sweet is the calm of Paradise the blest. *Alleluya!*

But lo! there breaks a yet more glorious day;
The Saints triumphant rise in bright array:
The King of Glory passes on His way. *Alleluya!*.

From earth's wide bounds, from ocean's farthest coast,
Through gates of pearl streams in the countless host,
Singing to Father, Son, and Holy Ghost. *Alleluya!*

William How

ANGEL OF GOD

ANGEL of God, my guardian dear,
To whom His love commits me here,
Ever this day be at my side,
To light and guard, to rule and guide.

Traditional

INDEX OF FIRST LINES

	PAGE
Adam lay y-bounden	214
A far croonin' is pullin' me away	169
Ah, what can ail thee, Knight at arms	132
A knight ther was, and that a worthy man	147
Alas, my love, you do me wrong	43
A little Saint best fits a little Shrine	31
All the world's a stage	35
All things bright and beautiful	211
All under the leaves and the leaves of life	215
And did those feet in ancient time	176
And look how many Grecian tents do stand	148
Angel of God, my guardian dear	237
A Nightingale that all day long	83
A Parrot, from the Spanish main	84
A silly young Cricket, accustomed to sing	157
As I was a-walking	203
A sunny shaft did I behold	16
A swarm of bees in May is worth a load of hay	30
Ave Maria! o'er the earth and sea	73
A was an Apple-Pie	26
Away, for we are ready to a man!	192
Blessed are the poor in Spirit	165
Blue bells, cockle shells	28
Breathes there the man, with soul so dead	169
But look, the morn, in russet mantle clad	71
But the souls of the righteous are in the hands of God	235
Bring flowers of the rarest	232
Calico Pie	61
Christmas is coming, the geese are getting fat	3
Close thine eyes, and sleep secure	161
Come away, come away, death	52
Come, cheer up, my lads, 'tis to glory we steer	174
Come down, O Christ, and help me! reach Thy hand	221
Come now, a roundel and a fairy song	127
Come, sons of summer, by whose toil	201
Crown Him with many crowns	226
Cuckoo, Cuckoo	17
Dear Lucy, you know what my wish is	47
Death be not proud, though some have called thee	53
Don't-Care—he didn't care	26

INDEX OF FIRST LINES

	PAGE
Drink to me only with thine eyes	44
D'ye ken John Peel with his coat so gay?	86
Earth has not anything to show more fair	178
Egypt's might is tumbled down	111
England with all thy faults, I love thee still—	178
Fair daffodils, we weep to see	82
'Farewell, rewards and fairies	144
Farewell to Old England forever	183
Father of All! In every Age	163
Fear no more the heat o' th' sun	54
Firmly I believe and truly	233
First it rained, and then it snew	3
For all the saints who from their labours rest	236
For I know that my redeemer liveth	212
For I will consider my cat Jeoffry	87
Forty days and forty nights	14
For want of a nail, the shoe is lost	159
From breakfast on through all the day	76
From ghoulies and ghosties and lang-legged beasties	32
Full many a glorious morning have I seen	72
Gay go up and gay go down	31
Give me a good digestion, Lord	159
Glory be to God for dappled things	82
God save our gracious Queen	179
Go forth upon thy journey, Christian soul!	235
Golden slumbers kiss your eyes	76
Good people all, of every sort	92
Great fleas have little fleas upon their backs to bite 'em	32
Guide me, O Thou great Redeemer	220
Half a league, half a league	103
Hail, Queen of Heaven, the ocean Star!	231
Hamelin Town's in Brunswick	149
Hark! she is call'd, the parting hour is come	229
Hark! when the night is falling	170
He clasps the crag with crooked hands	87
Here come six jolly miners	203
Here we come a-wassailing	9
He rises and begins to round	93
He thought he saw an Elephant	62
He which hath no stomach to this fight	117

	PAGE
Home, home from the horizon far and clear	75
How doth the little crocodile	87
How sweet the moonlight sleeps upon this bank!	75
I am monarch of all I survey	184
I bind unto myself today	217
I caught this morning morning's minion,	71
If I should die, think only this of me	121
If all the world were paper	57
If Candlemas be fair and bright	13
I found a house at Florence on the hill	191
If the oak is out before the ash	30
I had a dove, and the sweet dove died	95
I had a little nut-tree, nothing would it bear	61
I have seen old ships sail like swans asleep	186
I got me flowers to straw Thy way	14
I know a bank where the wild thyme blows	143
'I'll tell thee everything I can	66
I met a traveller from an antique land	187
In a cool curving world he lies	89
In Dublin's fair city	199
In Flanders fields the poppies blow	123
In the bleak mid-winter	4
In Xanadu did Kubla Khan	128
I sing of a maiden	5
I saw a fair maiden	5
I saw a peacock with a fiery tail	57
I saw a ship a-sailing	59
It is little I repair to the matches of the Southron folk	41
Jenny kiss'd me when we met	45
Lars Porsena of Clusium	106
Lavender's blue, dilly, dilly, lavender's green	41
Lead, Kindly Light, amid the encircling gloom	221
Let us now praise famous men	166
Lord, now lettest Thou Thy servant depart in peace	235
Love bade me welcome: yet my soul drew back	223
Matthew, Mark, Luke and John	74
Me name is Jim, the carter lad	197
Men of Harlech, march to glory	115
Much had I travell'd in the realms of gold	129
Multiplication is vexation	29

INDEX OF FIRST LINES

	PAGE
My duty to you both, on equal love	123
My little son, who look'd from thoughtful eyes	38
My song is love unknown	222
My soul doth magnify the Lord	228
My true love hath my heart, and I have his	43
My work is done	207
Nothing is so beautiful as spring	15
November Evenings! Damp and still	121
Now the hungry lion roars	143
O Bread of Heaven, beneath this veil	225
O dear me, what a pickle I'm in!	28
O God our help in ages past	234
Oh,—Paddy dear! an' did ye hear the news that's goin' round?	173
Oh to be in England	177
'Oh where are you going?' 'To Scarborough fair	133
O mistress mine, where are you roaming?	44
O my boat can sweetly float	198
O my Luve's like a red, red rose	45
Once more unto the breach, dear friends, once more	105
One I love, two I love	25
On either side the river lie	137
One summer evening…I found	37
On the first day of Christmas my true love sent to me	10
O saving Victim, opening wide	227
O sleep! it is a gentle thing	78
O then I see Queen Mab hath been with you	134
Our birth is but a sleep and a forgetting	36
Our King went forth to Normandy	104
Our second Eve puts on her mortal shroud	228
O what harper could worthily harp it	40
'O where have ye been, Lord Randall, my son?	142
'O where have ye been, my long, long love?	130
O Wild West Wind, thou breath of Autumn's being	20
O world invisible, we view thee	232
O worship the Lord in the beauty of holiness!	13
O young Lochinvar is come out of the west	47
Peter Piper picked a peck of pickled pepper	27
Praise to the Holiest in the height	219
Prayer the Church's banquet, Angels' age	220

	Page
Red sky at night	30
Ring out, wild bells, to the wild sky	12
Rosy apple, lemon or pear	27
Round the cape of a sudden came the sea	51
Same old slippers	30
Say not the struggle naught availeth	120
Season of mists and mellow fruitfulness	19
See amid the winter's snow	8
See the Kitten on the wall	18
She sate upon her Dobie	64
She walks in beauty, like the night	46
Should auld acquaintance be forgot	52
Sing a song of sixpence	25
Snowy, Flowy, Blowy	22
So she went into the garden	58
So, some tempestuous morn in early June	16
Soul of my Saviour, sanctify my breast	226
So, we'll go no more a-roving	51
Speed bonnie boat like a bird on the wing	171
Star light, star bright	73.
Still on the spot Lord Marmion stay'd	170
St. Swithin's Day, if thou dost rain	17
Sweet Suffolk Owl, so trimly dight	82
Teach me my God and King	207
Tell me not, Sweet, I am unkind	114
That's my last Duchess painted on the wall	49
That time of year thou mayst in me behold	19
The angels' eyes, whom veils cannot deceive	224
The ash grove how graceful, how plainly 'tis speaking	172
The Assyrian came down like the wolf on the fold	112
The Fox went out one wintry night	84
The grey sea and the long black land	50
The harp that once thro' Tara's halls	173
The heavens declare the glory of God	99
The holly and the ivy	7
The isles of Greece, the isles of Greece!	187
The Jackdaw sat on the Cardinal's chair!	96
The Lady Poverty was fair	162
The lion and the unicorn	57
The Lord is my shepherd	213
The Minstrel Boy to the war is gone	114
The mountain sheep are sweeter	112

INDEX OF FIRST LINES

	PAGE
The naked earth is warm with spring	122
The night has a thousand eyes	75
The Owl and the Pussy-Cat went to sea	65
The people that walked in darkness	213
The quality of mercy is not strain'd	147
The rain it raineth on the just	148
There is a green hill far away	216
There is a spot, 'mid barren hills	178
There was a lady in the West	136
There was a sound of revelry by night	119
There was three kings into the East	199
The sheets were frozen hard, and they cut the naked hand	11
The silver swan, who living had no note	87
The soote season, that bud and bloom forth brings	15
The spacious firmament on high	211
The splendour falls on castle walls	127
The world is charged with the grandeur of God	100
The year's at the spring	71
Thirty days hath September	30
This royal throne of kings, this scept'red isle	176
Thomas a Tittimus took two Ts	28
Thrice the brinded cat hath mew'd	135
Tiger! Tiger! burning bright	95
Tinker, tailor	27
'Tis the voice of the sluggard; I heard him complain—	158
To hear the lark begin his flight	72
'Twas a summer evening	118
'Twas brillig, and the slithy toves	59
'Twas on a lofty vase's side	91
Twinkle, twinkle, little bat!	57
Under a spreading chestnut tree	204
Under the greenwood tree	15
Under the wide and starry sky	53
Upon the King! Let us our lives, our souls	160
Welcome, all wonders in one sight!	6
We praise Thee, O God: we acknowledge Thee to be the Lord	218
Whan that Aprille with his shoures sote	183
Whatever course of Life great Jove allots	159
Whatever I do, and whatever I say	42
What is this that roareth thus?	29
What passing bells for those who die as cattle?	122
What wondrous life is this I lead!	81

	PAGE
When Britain first, at Heaven's command	175
When he killed the Mudjokivis	28
When icicles hang by the wall	3
When I was sick and lay a-bed	39
When lovely Woman stoops to folly	51
When soft September brings again	172
When the words rustle no more	74
When you're lying awake with a dismal headache	77
Where the bee sucks, there suck I	127
Where the pools are bright and deep	36
Wi' a hundred pipers, an' a', an' a'	116
'Will you walk a little faster?' said a whiting to a snail	60
Who can find a virtuous woman?	205
Who would true valour see	162
Yan, tan, tethera, methera	29
Ye that do your Master's will	163
Yin, twa, three	25
Young I am, and yet unskill'd	45
Your ghost will walk, you lover of trees	190

INDEX OF AUTHORS

PAGE

ADDISON, Joseph (1672-1719)
    The Spacious Firmament on High   211
ADY, Thomas (17th century)
    Before Sleeping (A Candle in the Dark)   74
ALEXANDER, Cecil Frances (1823-95)
    All things bright and beautiful   211
    Calvary   216
    St Patrick's Breastplate
        (based on a hymn of St Patrick)   217
ANONYMOUS
    A Peacock with a fiery tail   57
    A Ship a-sailing   59
    If all the World were Paper   57
    Maths   29
    My Little Nut-Tree   61
    Prayer (found in Chester Cathedral)   159
    Runaway Daughter   27
    The Agincourt Song   104
    The Ant and the Cricket   157
    The Bells of London   31
    The Modern Hiawatha   28
    The Silver Swan (set by Orlando Gibbons)   87
    Thomas a Tittimus   28
    What a Pickle I'm in   28
ARNOLD, Matthew (1822-88)
    Summer (Thyrsis)   16

PAGE

BALLADS
    Farewell to Old England forever
        (popular ballad based on a street song)   183
    John Barleycorn, version by Robert Burns   199
    Lord Randall   142
    Scarborough Fair (version of the Elfin Knight)   133
    The Demon Lover   130
    The Devil's Nine Questions   136

BARHAM, Richard Harris (1788-1845)
    The Jackdaw of Rheims   96

BIBLE, The Holy (King James' version & Apocrypha)
    In the Hands of God (Wisdom of Solomon)   235
    Let us now praise famous men (Ecclesiasticus)   166
    Our Lady's Song—Magnificat
        (St Luke's Gospel)   228
    Psalm Nineteen (The Psalms)   99
    Simeon's Song—Nunc Dimittis
        (St Luke's Gospel)   235
    The Beatitudes (St Matthew's Gospel)   165
    The Faith of Job (Job)   212
    The Fruit of her Hands (Proverbs)   205
    The Lord is my Shepherd (Psalm 23)   213
    The People that walked in Darkness (Isaiah)   213

BLAKE, William (1757-1827)
    Jerusalem   176
    The Tiger   95

BOURDILLON, Francis William (1852-1921)
    The Night has a thousand Eyes (Light)   75

INDEX OF AUTHORS

PAGE

BOWEN, Charles, Lord (1835-94)
    Justice   148
BRIDGES, Matthew (1800-94)
    Crown Him with many Crowns   226
BRONTE, Emily (1818-48)
    The Hearth of Home   178
BROOKE, Rupert (1887-1915)
    The Fish   89
    The Soldier   121
BROWNING, Elizabeth Barrett (1806-61)
    Florence   191
BROWNING, Robert (1812-89)
    'De Gustibus—'   190
    Home Thoughts from Abroad   177
    Meeting at Night   50
    My last Duchess   49
    Parting at Morning   51
    Pippa's Song (Pippa Passes)   71
    The Pied Piper of Hamelin   149
BUNYAN, John (1628-88)
    To be a Pilgrim   162
BURNS, Robert (1759-96)
    A red, red, rose   45
    Auld lang syne   52
    John Barleycorn, version of the ballad   199
BYRON, George Gordon, Lord (1788-1824)
    She walks in Beauty   46
    The Angelus (Don Juan)   73

	PAGE
BYRON (continued)	
The Destruction of Sennacherib	112
The Eve of the Battle of Waterloo	
(Childe Harold's Pilgrimage)	119
The Isles of Greece (Don Juan)	187
We'll go no more a-roving	51
CALVERLEY, Charles Stuart (1831-84)	
The Schoolmaster: abroad with his Son	40
CAMPBELL, Thomas (1777-1844)	
The Parrot: a true Story	84
CAROLS	
Adam (mediæval)	214
I sing of a maiden (15th century)	5
Lullay, my liking (15th century)	5
The Holly and the Ivy	7
CARROLL, Lewis (1832-98)	
A-Sitting on a Gate	66
Jabberwocky	59
The Little Crocodile	87
The Lobster Quadrille	60
The Mad Gardener's Song	62
Twinkle, twinkle, little bat	57
CASWALL, Edward (1814-78)	
See amid the Winter's Snow	8

INDEX OF AUTHORS

PAGE

CHAUCER, Geoffrey (1343-1400)
    The Knight   147
    Pilgrimages to Canterbury   183
        (both from the Prologue to the Canterbury Tales)

CLOUGH, Arthur Hugh (1819-61)
    Pont-y-Wern: Denbighshire   172
    Say not the Struggle naught availeth   120

COLERIDGE, Mary Elizabeth (1861-1907)
    Egypt's Might   111

COLERIDGE, Samuel Taylor (1772-1834)
    Kubla Khan   128
    Song   16
    Sleep (The Rime of the Ancient Mariner)   78

CORBETT, Richard (1582-1635)
    The Fairies' Farewell   144

COWPER, William (1731-1800)
    England (The Task)   178
    The Nightingale and the Glow-Worm   83
    Verses of Alexander Selkirk   184

CRASHAW, Richard (1612/13-49)
    A Hymn of the Nativity   6
    On the Glorious Assumption of Our Blessed Lady   229

CROSSMAN, Samuel (1624-84)
    Love Unknown   222

DECKER, Thomas (1570-1641)
    Golden Slumbers   76

	Page
de MORGAN, Augustus (1806-71)	
Fleas	32
DONNE, John (1571-1631)	
Death (Divine Poems)	53
DRYDEN, John (1631-1700)	
Song for a Girl (Love Triumphant)	45
ELLIS, George (1753-1815)	
The Twelve Months	22
FLECKER, James Elroy (1884-1915)	
November Eves	121
Stillness	74
The Golden Journey to Samarkand (Hassan)	192
The Old Ships	186
FOOTE, Samuel (1720-77)	
The Great Panjandrum	58
GARRICK, David (1717-79	
Heart of Oak	174
GILBERT, William Schwenck, Sir (1836-1911)	
A Nightmare	77
GODLEY, Alfred Dennis (1859-1925)	
Motor Bus	29
GOLDSMITH, Oliver (1728-74)	
An Elegy on the Death of a Mad Dog	92
Woman	51

INDEX OF AUTHORS

GRAVES, John Woodcock (1794-1886)
    John Peel — 86

GRAY, Thomas (1716-71)
    On a favourite Cat drowned — 91

GRENFELL, Julian (1888-1915)
    Into Battle — 122

HERBERT, George (1593-1633)
    Easter — 14
    Love — 223
    Prayer — 220
    The Elixir — 207

HERRICK, Robert (1591-1674)
    Ternary of Littles — 31
    The Hock Cart: Harvest Home — 201
    To Daffodils — 82

HICKSON, William Edward (1803-70)
    God Save the Queen (additional stanzas) — 179

HOGG, James (1770-1835)
    A Boy's Song — 36

HOLMES, Oliver Wendell (1809-94)
    Aunt Tabitha — 42

HOPKINS, Gerard Manley (1844-89)
    God's Grandeur — 100
    Pied Beauty — 82
    Spring — 15
    The Windhover: to Christ our Lord — 71

	PAGE

HOW, William Walsham (1823-97)
    For all the Saints   236
HUNT, James Henry Leigh (1784-1859)
    Jenny kiss'd Me   45
HYMNS
    Bring Flowers of the rarest   232
    Magnificat (Our Lady's Song)   228
    Nunc Dimittis (Simeon's Song)   235
    O Saving Victim
        (version of a hymn of St Thomas Aquinas)   227
    Soul of my Saviour (version of a mediæval hymn)   226
    We Praise Thee, O God—*Te Deum Laudamus*   218

JOHNSON, Samuel (1709-84)
    Festina Lente   159
JONSON, Ben (1573-1637)
    Song to Celia   44

KEATS, John (1795-1821)
    La Belle Dame sans Merci   132
    On first looking into Chapman's Homer   129
    Song   95
    To Autumn   19

LAMPTON, William (1859-1917)
    June Weddings   30

LEAR, Edward (1812-88)
    Calico Pie   61
    The Owl and the Pussy-Cat   65
    The Cummerbund: An Indian Poem   64

LINGARD, John, (1771-1851)
    Hail, Queen of Heaven   231

LONGFELLOW, Henry (1807-82)
    The Village Blacksmith   204

LOVELACE, Richard (1618-58)
    To Lucasta, on going to the Wars   114

MACAULAY, Thomas Babington, Lord (1800-59)
    Horatius (Lays of Ancient Rome)   106

MACRAE, John (1872-1918)
    In Flanders Fields   123

MARVELL, Andrew (1621-78)
    The Garden   81

MEREDITH, George (1828-1909)
    The Lark Ascending   93

MEYNELL, Alice (1847-1922)
    At Night   75
    The Lady Poverty   162

MILTON, John (1608-74)
    The Coming of Day (L'Allegro)   72

MONSELL, John Samuel Bewley (1811-75)
    Epiphany   13

	PAGE

MOORE, Thomas, (1779-1852)
    The Harp that once thro' Tara's Halls ... 173
    The Minstrel Boy ... 114

NAIRNE, Carolina, Lady (1766-1845)
    The Hundred Pipers ... 116

NEWMAN, John Henry, Cardinal (1801-90)
    Faith ... 233
    Praise to the Holiest ... 219
    The Song of the Guardian Angel ... 207
        (all the above from 'The Dream of Gerontius')
    The Pillar of the Cloud ... 221

OWEN, Wilfrid (1893-1918)
    Anthem for doomed Youth ... 122

OXENFORD, John (1812-77)
    Men of Harlech:
        (English words of Rhyfelgyrch gwyr Harlech) ... 115
    The Ash Grove (English words of Llwyn On) ... 172

PATMORE, Coventry (1823-96)
    The Toys ... 38

PEACOCK, Thomas Love (1785-1866)
    The War-Song of Dinas Vawr ... 112

POPE, Alexander (1688-1744)
    The Universal Prayer ... 163

INDEX OF AUTHORS

PAGE

ROSSETTI, Christina (1834-94)
    A Christmas Carol — 4

SCOTT, Walter, Sir (1771-1832)
    Edinburgh from the Pentland Hills — 170
    My Native Land — 169
        (both from the Lay of the Last Minstrel)
    Young Lochinvar (Ballad from Marmion) — 47

SHAKESPEARE, William (1564-1616)
    Ariel's Song (The Tempest) — 127
    Dawn (Hamlet) — 71
    Feste's Song (Twelfth Night) — 52
    King Henry, to his troops before Harfleur (Henry V) — 105
    King Henry on Responsibility (Henry V) — 160
    Mercy (The Merchant of Venice) — 147
    Moonlight at Belmont (The Merchant of Venice) — 75
    O Mistress Mine (Twelfth Night) — 44
    Order (Troilus and Cressida) — 148
    Puck describes the Fairies' favourite Time
        (A Midsummer Night's Dream) — 143
    Queen Mab (Romeo and Juliet) — 134
    Song (As You like It) — 15
    Sonnet Seventy-Three — 19
    Sonnet Thirty-Three — 72
    Titania's Orders (A Midsummer Night's Dream) — 127
    The Duke of Burgundy praises Peace (Henry V) — 123
    The Fairy Queen's Bed
        (A Midsummer Night's Dream) — 143

	Page
SHAKESPEARE, William (continued)	
The Song of Guiderius and Arviragus (Cymbeline)	54
The Seven Ages (As You Like It)	35
The Witches' Cauldron (Macbeth)	135
This Scept'red Isle (Richard II)	176
Upon Saint Crispin's Day (Henry V)	117
Winter (Love's Labour's Lost)	3
SHELLEY, Percy Bysshe (1792-1822)	
Ode to the West Wind	20
Ozymandias	187
SIDNEY, Philip, Sir (1543-86)	
The Bargain	43
SMART, Christopher (1722-71)	
Cat Jeoffry	88
SMYTTAN, George Hunt (1825-70)	
Lent	14
SOUTHEY, Robert (1774-1843)	
After Blenheim	118
SOUTHWELL, Robert, Saint & Martyr (1561-95)	
Of the Blessed Sacrament of the Altar	224
The Conception of Our Lady	228
STEVENSON, Robert Louis (1850-94)	
Christmas at Sea	11
Requiem	53
The Land of Counterpane	39
The Land of Nod	76
STUART, Charles, King Charles I (1600-49)	
On a quiet Conscience	161

INDEX OF AUTHORS

PAGE

SURREY, Henry Howard, Earl of (?1517-47)
    Description of Spring   15

TENNYSON, Alfred, Lord (1809-92)
    Blow, Bugle, Blow (The Princess)   127
    New Year (In Memoriam)   12
    The Charge of the Light Brigade   103
    The Eagle   87
    The Lady of Shalott   137

THACKERAY, William (1811-63)
    Persicos Odi   47

THOMPSON, Francis (1859-1907)
    At Lords   41
    The Kingdom of God   232

THOMSON, James (1700-48
    Rule Britannia (Masque of Alfred)   175

TRADITIONAL
    Angel of God   237
    Apple-Pie   26
    Bees   30
    Blue Bells, Cockle Shells   28
    Candlemas Day: 2nd February   13
    Cherry Stones   27
    Christmas is Coming   3
    Cockles and Mussels   199
    Cold weather   3
    Cuckoo   17
    Days in the Month   30

PAGE

TRADITIONAL (continued)

Don't Care	26
For the Dying or Departed	235
Ghoulies and Ghosties	32
God save the Queen	179
Greensleeves	43
Jim, the Carter Lad	197
Lavender's blue	41
Little Things	159
Petals	25
Peter Piper	27
Scotland the Brave	170
Sheep Counting	29
Sing a Song of Sixpence	25
Six Jolly Miners	203
Star Light, Star Bright	73
St Swithin's Day: 15th July	17
The Fox	84
The Lion and the Unicorn	57
The Pretty Ploughboy	203
The Queen of Connemara	198
The Road to the Isles	169
The Seven Virgins	215
The Skye Boat Song	171
The Twelve Days of Christmas	10
The Wearin' o' the Green	173
The Weather	30
Trees	30

INDEX OF AUTHORS

PAGE

TRADITIONAL (continued)
    Yin Twa Three (Scottish)   25
    Wassail Song   9

VAUGHAN, Edward (1827-1908)
    Bread of Heaven
        (Based on a Hymn of St Alphonsus Liguori)   225

VAUTOR, Thomas (16th/17th century)
    Sweet Suffolk Owl   82

WATTS, Isaac (1674-1748)
    O God our Help in Ages past   234
    The Sluggard   158

WESLEY, Charles (1707-88)
    The Joy of Sins forgiven (Short Hymns on Passages of Holy Scripture)   163

WILDE, Oscar (1854-1900)
    E Tenebris (Out of the Darkness)   221

WILLIAMS, William (1717-91)
    Guide me, O Thou Great Redeemer
        (English word of Arglwydd arwain trwy'r anialwch)   220

WORDSWORTH, William (1770-1850)
    A Boat at Night
        (The Prelude: Childhood and Schooltime)   37
    Composed upon Westminster Bridge   178
    Growing Up (Intimations of Immortality : Recollections of Early Childhood)   36
    The Kitten and falling Leaves   18

OTHER BOOKS FROM FISHER PRESS
All books are illustrated with line drawings

JOHN HENRY NEWMAN
Collected Poems & The Dream of Gerontius

Centenary edition of the poems of one of Britain's most significant 19th century figures, whose influence continues to grow; includes many favourite poems such as 'Lead Kindly Light' and 'Praise to the Holiest.'
176 pages   £6.99   ISBN 1 874037 02 7

FRANCIS THOMPSON
Collected Poems

One of Britain's finest mystical poets who glimpsed the 'many slendoured thing' while living rough on the London streets in the 1880s and '90s. This is the first paperback edition of the author of 'The Hound of Heaven.'
314 pages   £6.99   ISBN 1 874037 03 5

WILLIAM COBBETT
A History of the Protestant Reformation
with an introduction by Molly Townsend

After an extensive study of the historical evidence, Cobbett, the author of *Rural Rides*, concludes that the British public had been skilfully deceived about the nature of the Reformation. It was 'not the work of virtue, fanaticism, error, or ambition, but of love of plunder.' Readers will recognise the prejudices which much traditional history has imparted, and will be caught up with the broad sweep of Cobbett's gripping story.
272 pages   £8.99   ISBN 1 874037 10 8

ANTONY MATTHEW
Pearl of Great Price

Practical Guide to joining the Catholic Church and living today according to its teachings by a former British diplomat. Orthodox companion to the path taken by Newman, Chesterton, Ronald Knox, Alec Guiness, Evelyn Waugh, Malcolm Muggeridge, Muriel Spark and many others.
176 pages   £5.95   ISBN 1 874037 01 9

G K CHESTERTON
Autobiography

"...the voice speaks from the page entirely without malice. The reader might be sitting across the fireside from him."
The Sunday Telegraph

"...Chesterton's wonderfully engaging Autobiography is made all the more attractive by Mary Tyler's evocative illustrations, and by William Oddie's Introduction which latter underlines 'the simple and valiant holiness of a man whose life was one long, glorious argument with the Age.'"
The Salisbury Review

362 Pages   £9.99   ISBN 1 874037 04 3

G K CHESTERTON
A Short History of England

G K Chesterton's classic account of English history written for the ordinary reader. It shows how the rights of the common people were progressively taken from them by a land hungry élite. Full of Chestertonian wit, prophetic insight and love of England.

"...Chesterton is at once the most concise and fullest historian."
The Observer

192 pages   £6.99   ISBN 1 874037 09 4

BERNARD HOLLAND
Memoir of Kenelm Digby

Account of the life and writing of the author of *The Broadstone of Honour*, who fired Britain with fresh enthusiasm for the moral ideals of chivalry. There is again renewed interest in Digby's ideas, which influenced "The Young England" group of the early Victorian period, the Gothic revival, and the values of the boy scout movement. Holland's memoir tells of Digby's travels on foot all over Europe just after the Napoleonic wars, his invention of the modern rowing eight, his vast learning, his circle of friends in England and France, and of his tender marriage and family life shaped by his romantic ideals.

242 pages   £4.99   ISBN 1 874037 05 1

HUGH DORMER, D.S.O
War Diary
with a facsimile of a leaf from his secret diary, maps, military sketch plan, and a previously unpublished account of two naval operations in the English Channel

Nothing in World War II fiction captures the excitement and terror of the exploits of the Special Operations Executive—the predecessor of the S.A.S—so well as Hugh Dormer's diary of 15 months in 1943-44. He was twice parachuted into France—leading small bands of men to dynamite key installations of the German military machine— escaping by hazardous night treks over the Pyrenees into Spain. The climate of fear under which the French lived during the German occupation is powerfully conveyed. The diary concludes with an account of the D day landings when Dormer had rejoined his beloved Irish guardsmen, and with the armoured push into Normandy in which this brilliant and heroic young writer was killed.
156 pages   £7.99   ISBN 1 874037 11 6

ROBERT HUGH BENSON
Confessions of a Convert

Sensational account of how the son of an Archbishop of Canterbury left Anglican orders to become a Catholic priest and a successful novelist. The younger brother of E F and A C Benson, he provides sharp portraits of his eccentric family and Edwardian contemporaries.

"...His apology for his decision makes enthralling reading and he fights his corner with the utmost eloquence."
The Daily Telegraph
128 pages   £4.99   ISBN 1 874037 00 0

HELEN JACKSON
Ramona

Magnificent classic American novel about the eviction of the Californian Indians from their land by the American settlers who went West. Helen Jackson was a friend of Harriet Becher Stowe: *Ramona* had a similar effect on the American public in relation to the treatment of Indians as *Uncle Tom's Cabin* did for that of the American negro. A passionate tale of a half-Indian girl whose love for a

dispossessed Indian sheep shearer shatters the serene world of the Spanish ranch on which she lives.
416 pages   £8.99   ISBN 1 874037 07 8

F MARION CRAWFORD
The Heart of Rome

One of the finest novels of this great story teller of the 1890s and Edwardian period. The aristocratic Conti family are in danger of losing their palazzo in the heart of Rome. Their overspending and the collapse of the property market have caught up with them. The prospect of a suitable marriage for their lovely daughter, Donna Sabina, is now remote. But a mysterious young archaelogist rents an appartment in the palazzo to discover its strange history; in the process he uncovers 'the secret of the lost waters.' A web of violence and intrigue brings the two young people together in one of Crawford's most fast moving stories of Roman High Society. The perfect book for an Italian holiday.

"…cleverly paced tale of princely virtue triumphant over plebeian skulduggery.'

The Times Literary Supplement

COVENTRY PATMORE
The Bow set in the Cloud

A collection of his most important writing on literature, art and architecture, moral life, politics, women & religion. Patmore was the author of 'The Angel in the House', a very popular long poem which defined the Victorian attitude to love and marriage. His great intelligence and the width of his interests give him a good claim to be considered as the most formidable intellect among Victorian men of letters, as well as the least "politically correct." Roger Scruton has recently drawn attention to the originality of his writing on architecture; Sir Herbert Read believed that his later writing, which is included in this collection, is comparable with that of Pascal's *Pensées*.
224 pages   £8.99   ISBN 1 874037 13 2